Boy's Sailor Suit
The Delineator, September 1885.

COVER PHOTO: 19in (48.3cm) German bisque reproduction Heubach doll by Opal Butler, costumed by Hazel Ulseth. Ball-jointed body, stationary eyes and human hair wig. Dressed in a blue cotton sailor suit of 1885 style with bloused top, slightly flared pants closed with a fall front and a soft-brimmed sailor hat completing the costume. **Right:** 17in (43.2cm) German bisque reproduction doll by Marianne De Nunez, costumed by Hazel Ulseth. All-jointed body, stationary eyes and human hair wig. Dressed in a boy's kilt of 1888 style in two shades of silk, dark brown and beige, with 33 buttons used for trim. A reefer cap is brown leather, matching the brown leather boots. *Photograph by Marty Ulseth.*

Boys' Fashions 1885 to 1905

Chronicle for Costume Historians and Doll Costumers

Compiled by Donna H. Felger

Introduction and patterns for two period outfits.
Hats, outer and under garments and shoe patterns by Hazel Ulseth & Helen Shannon.

Boy's Kilt Dress
The Delineator, November 1888.

Published By  **HOBBY HOUSE PRESS, INC.**
Cumberland, Maryland 21502

TABLE OF CONTENTS

INTRODUCTION
by **Helen Shannon** and **Hazel Ulseth**

Boys seem to be more or less neglected in the world of dolls, both in the area of doll production during the early years of manufacture and as a natural consequence of this fact, in the area of costuming as well. This book makes an effort to narrow that gap in dressing boy dolls and to provide a pictorial progression of types of clothing worn by boys during the 1880 to 1905 period, and even offers two fold-out patterns designed by Hazel Ulseth and Helen Shannon to give costumers a good start in dressing their perhaps neglected boy dolls correctly.

This book supplements and complements *Antique Children's Fashions, 1880-1900* by Hazel Ulseth and Helen Shannon, published by Hobby House Press, Inc. (1982), which relates primarily to costuming girl dolls, but includes a few brief references to boys' costumes. In any case, many of the techniques and sewing methods covered in *Antique Children's Fashions, 1880-1900* apply equally to all kinds of costuming and should be of help, not only in the technical aspects of sewing, but also in the philosophical approach.

We have always believed that clothing original to the doll wearing an outfit is preferable, but still face with pragmatism the fact that very few good costumes survive the wear and tear of the intervening years since such dolls were originally dressed. So we look again to fashion magazines of the period to determine what styles were common to the period of the doll's manufacture, or we are perhaps fortunate to have the original costume available ... even though tattered and worn ... to copy.

Changes in boys' styles were less extreme than those changes which occurred in girls' and women's clothing. The males of the human species have reversed the traditional pattern found in the bird and animal kingdoms where the males inherit all the lovely wild bright colors and striking forms while the females remain relatively unobtrusive in their dull and lifeless colors.

Instead we note, at least in the last hundred years or so that grays, browns, blacks and navy blues and other sombre colors seem to have dominated male attire. Of course, during one period (1887 to 1900) one departure from this sombre attire will delight many costumers ... the lavish use of lace on boys' blouses and suits, particularly apparent during the "Little Lord Fauntleroy" period which followed publication of the book by that name, a book unaccountably illustrated in styles prominent during the cavalier and Van Dyke period. So, as distressing as it must have been to little boys of the time to appear "costumed" in black velvet suits, white silk blouses dripping with lace, a smashing brilliant red sash with fringe and horrors! ... topped by a picturesque plumed hat ... it is nevertheless the costumer's delight, and one suspects that the boy dolls will not raise much of a protest if such an outfit is made at the whim of a costumer. Toward the end of the 1890s, brighter colors began to appear in boys' suits — green, purple and wine being among the colors recommended by fashion designers for boys' wear.

Throughout the 1880s and 1890s, boys of two to six years wore kilts with tailored jackets; for the most part, older boys wore tailored suits with short tight pants and boys of all ages looked forward eagerly to their first "long pants," a long period of anticipation, indeed, since that momentous occasion would not materialize until about age sixteen.

In the latter part of this period both kilts and suits were often embellished with wide collars, much-ruffled fronts and full sleeves. A popular variation in boys' suits was the sailor suit with its picturesque adaptation of a sailor's uniform hat and the blouse accorded the name "middy" after the midshipmen from whom it was adopted. In fact, sailor suits were popular in various versions of this style for both boys and girls over a long period, starting in the 1880s and even recently we have seen a brief revival of sailor suits in our own current fashion books for both adults and children. References made to other mariners' styles include the pea jacket, the reefer and the Norfolk jacket. As with many fashions, these styles come and go and while we still find sailor suits and middy blouses popular, we doubt if many boys now would put up with the long curls and fussy clothing of the Lord Fauntleroy period.

Hats, in general, varied from a small plain visored cap to a wide-brimmed straw hat with flowing ribbons, to small pill-box types and to the full-crowned, large-visored caps worn by seamen in the 19th century. Some specific variations which appear in fashion books include the tam-o-shanter, the Scotch cap, which was worn by both boys and girls, the Turkish hat with long tassel and many variations of berets.

Shoes were frequently high and buttoned or laced miniatures of men's boots, black or brown, and were usually worn with black ribbed stockings, although with sailor suits vertically striped stockings were acceptable. We also find leggings shown as an adjunct to a small boy's outfit, in varying lengths from mid-calf to above the knees. Of course, Lord Fauntleroy suits, in keeping with the period, were worn with patent leather pumps or other types of slippers, over which leggings were sometimes worn.

Underwear apparently consisted (from the brief references we have found) of a simple knit shirt or balbriggan (a type of woolen or cotton knit) with sleeves, long or short, depending on the season, and balbriggan pants, with long or short legs depending on the exigencies of the weather. Union suits were available for both sexes of all ages.

Transition was being made during the 1880s and 1890s to a standard fly-front for boys and men, although many pants were still made with fall-fronts. The 19in (48.3cm) pattern included in this book has a typical fall-front.

Customarily, boys up to the age of two were dressed in the same type of clothing as that worn by girls and as already mentioned, from age two years to five or six years, they wore "kilts," a term which designated a skirted suit with a somewhat tailored jacket, varying from a simple style to one with many tailored details. Your fold-out pattern is such an example. From kilts small boys were "breeched," a term used to mark the transition from kilts to pants. And then our small boy of five or six years wore his short tight pants, simply tailored, or later ruffled blouses and tailored jackets in eager anticipation of the next step in growing up. And behold! We have planned that next step by including a manly little sailor suit with long-flared pants and a jaunty sailor hat.

So the customer will have to decide how old she wants her boy dolls to be and that decision will lead her in the direction of a proper selection of costume. From the basic patterns given here to fit dolls 17in (43.2cm) and 19in (48.3cm), demonstrating a kilt and a sailor suit, there are many possible variations available through the simple expedient of consulting the many authentic costumes in this book which cover the period from 1885 to 1905. Many distinctive tailoring details may be easily adapted to the fold-out patterns in this book and two pages of reprints from *The Delineator*, December 1892, will demonstrate the methods for embroiding nautical emblems for middy blouses. And do not forget that the boys dressed in sailor suits may have a little sister wearing a similar outfit so, by using the middy top given and by adding a pleated skirt, another pattern may easily be developed.

Let us all get to work on the heretofore, much neglected, boy dolls awaiting our tender care; our costuming expertise should be greatly enhanced by the material assembled in this book.

Front View.

Front View.   Back View.

Back View.

1888 Boy Doll Costume

Illustration 1. Navy blue flannel is the material pictured in this instance and braid forms the decoration. The trousers are shaped by seams along the inside and outside of the legs and at the center of the front and back, and by a dart at either side of the center seam of the back. The outside seams are left open for a short distance from the top. Over each is laid a row of braid that is continued to the top. In front of it a similar row is placed. A band is sewn to the top of the front and back and the trousers are closed at the sides.

The blouse is in true sailor style and is shaped by side and shoulder seams. It is gathered along the lower edge and finished with a belt. The blouse and trousers are connected by buttons and buttonholes; the blouse droops in sailor fashion over the belt. The fronts of the blouse are closed with buttons and buttonholes. To the neck at the back is joined a sailor collar that falls deep and square at the back and is joined to the fronts at either side of the closing. The ends of the collar meet some distance below the neck under the jaunty sailor tie which is formed of braid fastened under the collar and tied in a sailor knot. Two rows of braid trim the edges of the collar and three rows trim the wrists of the coat sleeves.

The cap is formed by a round crown piece and four shaped sections which form the sides. The sections are joined together and a straight band is fitted to the head and joins the lower edge of the side sections. The band is covered with a row of braid which is turned to form a point and then allowed to form short streamers at the back.

To be perfectly happy, a boy doll must have a jaunty sailor suit which he may wear during play hours. This set contains exactly the kind of garments necessary for such a suit. White, cream, blue and striped flannels will be used for these suits, white and cream being especially dainty. Braid or fancy stitching will be the usual trimming but often the suit will be finished plainly. Embroidered anchors, stars, oars and so forth will decorate the suit of an oarsman or sailor doll.

Pattern No. 116, *The Delineator,* **November 1888.**

1888 Boy Doll Sailor Suit

Illustration 2. This boy doll is suitably attired for yachting, sailing and so forth, looking both stylish and pretty. Navy blue and white flannel were chosen for making the suit with white braid for trimming. The

trousers extend only to the knees; each outside leg seam is defined by a row of white braid.

The blouse fits smoothly across the shoulders and droops in true sailor fashion over the belt that finishes its gathered lower edge. The white flannel sailor collar falls square at the back, its pointed ends meeting some distance below the throat. A trimming of crosswise rows of white braid is visible between its flaring edges in front. Tiny ribbon ties are placed at the ends of the collar. The coat sleeves are trimmed with cuff facings of white flannel.

The cap is of the style worn by sailors. The sides are shaped to join a round crown and about the band is placed a white ribbon that falls in streamers at the back.

Twilled flannel, serge, cloth and other wool goods may be selected for making this suit. Black, white or blue braid or narrow ribbon may be used for trimming. A sailor's knot of ribbon or surah may be placed below the collar which may be trimmed with rows of braid or embroidered with stars, anchors, crossed oars, capstans and so forth. Metal emblems may be applied, if liked, and metal buttons used in closing. Buttons will often be used for trimming instead of braid.

Pattern No. 116, *The Delineator,* **November 1888.**

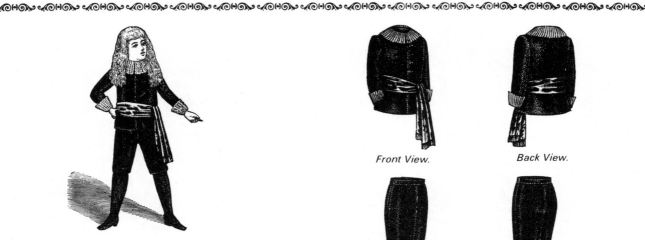

Front View.   Back View.

Front View.   Back View.

1889 Boy Doll Fauntleroy Suit

Illustration 3. This set consists of a boy doll's Fauntleroy jacket, sash and trousers. The jacket and trousers are made of black velvet here and the sash of crimson silk. Fauntleroy ruffs of white lace are worn at the neck and wrists. The fronts of the jacket are united to the back by shoulder and underarm seams, then rendered shapely by a well-curved center seam. An invisible closing is effected at the center of the front with buttons and buttonholes in a fly or with hooks and eyes; the lower outline is uniform. The sleeves are in coat-sleeve style. The sash of crimson silk is tied about the waist and hangs in long fringed ends at the left side with picturesque effect.

The trousers are shaped by the customary seams and hip darts. They extend to the knees and are finished at the top with waistbands and closed at each side with a button and buttonhole.

Rough or smooth finished cloths in dark blue, brown, green, gray or black, striped checked or mixed suitings, corduroy or velveteen may be selected for making these little suits. The sash may be of any soft bright-colored silk and deeply fringed at the ends. Cashmere or any soft wool goods may be used for the sash. Black silk stockings and black slippers are worn.

Pattern No. 124, *The Delineator,* **November 1889.**

1889 Boy Doll Costume

Illustration 4. This boy doll's Norfolk suit comes in seven sizes for boy dolls from 12in (30.5cm) to 24in (61cm). In this instance striped cheviot was selected for the jacket and trousers and chamois for the leggings. The jacket is fitted with underarm seams and a center seam and is closed at the center of the front to the waistline where it is encircled by a belt, the edges of which are followed by a single row of stitching. A broad box plait is laid on each front back of the closing. At each side of the center seam is arranged a similar plait. A row of stitching is made just above the lower edge. A deep cuff is simulated with stitching on each of

Front View.   Back View.

Front View.   Back View.

the shapely coat sleeves. At the neck is a standing collar which is also decorated along its free edges with a row of stitching.

The trousers are shaped by the customary seams and are finished at the top with waistbands that are fastened at each side with a button and buttonhole.

Each legging is fitted by a seam at the front and at the back of the leg and extends in a deep point over the instep, being held in place by a narrow strap passed beneath the foot in front of the heel and joined to the lower edge at each side.

Smooth-faced cloth, corkscrew, diagonal and various fancy suitings will be chosen for suits of this kind. A plain finish is usually preferred, although braid binding and fancy buttons may be added when in keeping with the material.

Pattern No. 128, *The Delineator,* **December 1889.**

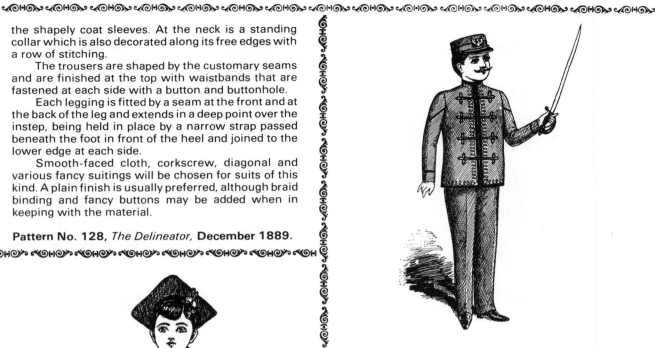

1899 Captain Doll

Illustration 6. Captain Doll is a very handsome brown-haired gentleman 18in (45.7cm) high. He is clad in a suit of army gray cloth with black braid trimmings and cunning little bell buttons of gilt. His trim moustache is made of hair to match that on his head. The cap and sword, also a tiny knapsack, were purchased in a set at a toy store.

The Designer, **December 1899.**

1899 Master Dewey Doll

Illustration 5. Master Dewey Doll is a 14in (35.6cm) handsome little sailor laddie. He has brown hair which has been brushed until it lays smooth. He wears a suit of white duck trimmed with narrow scarlet braid and has a tie of scarlet silk. His stockings are scarlet and his shoes black kid. His cap is made of white duck with a scarlet band and tassels. *Master Dewey* has another suit which he will wear on state occasions. It is a Fauntleroy costume of blue velvet with a deep collar. The shirt and cuffs of white lawn are trimmed with Swiss embroidery. For this costume he has blue silk stockings and patent leather slippers.

The Designer, **December 1899.**

1905 Boy Doll Sailor Suit

Illustration 7. A boy doll's sailor suit.

Pattern No. 3339, *The Designer,* **December 1905.**

1905 Boy Doll Costume

Illustration 8. A boy doll's costume for dressy occasions.

Pattern No. 3339, *The Designer,* **December 1905.**

1905 Boy Doll Costumes

Illustration 9. This set consists of a cadet suit of coat and trousers, a middy suit of blouse and trousers and an "Uncle Sam" outfit of vest, coat and trousers. The last are generally used for dressing knit or rag dolls. This set is cut in sizes suitable for dolls from 12in (30.5cm) to 24in (61cm).

Pattern No. 4639, *The Designer,* **December 1905.**

1906 Boy Doll Sailor Suit

Illustration 10. The fitted blouse of this boy doll's sailor suit is finished with a casing and drawstring. The one-seamed sleeve is completed by a band cuff and a sailor collar and removable shield are provided. The knickerbockers are fitted by center back and front seams, also inside leg seams, the lower edges being finished with casings and elastics.

Pattern No. 2102, *The Designer,* **December 1906.**

Front View.   *Back View.*

1886 Costume

Illustration 11. For the very wee man between two and six years old this is an exceedingly handsome little costume. It is developed in mixed cloth and very effectively trimmed with braid and buttons. The skirt comprises two plain front sections and a kilted back section. The front sections lap broadly and are closed with buttonholes and buttons in the same manner as a double-breasted garment. They are hemmed and bound all round, except at the top, with braid and are lapped over the back section to which they are joined. The skirt is joined to the lower edge of a well-shaped supporting waist which buttons in front.

The jacket is shaped to cling gracefully to the form by underarm darts and center and side seams that terminate below the waistline, the back skirt forming two pretty tabs. The jacket fronts are cut away to expose a vest that is somewhat shorter and extends to the underarm darts. The vest closes all the way down with buttonholes and buttons. All the loose edges of the jacket and vest are bound with braid. The fronts are decorated with strips of braid that extend from under the binding and are turned in points a little further back under buttons. Pocket laps bound with braid are sewn to the fronts. The coat sleeves are trimmed in cuff outline with a row of doubled braid, a pointed strap formed of the braid extending forward from the outside seam and decorated at the point with a button. The collar resembles the sailor style at the back and is fancifully shaped in front. All its edges are bound with braid.

Fancy and plain suitings of all kinds, also tricots, cheviots, serges, cloths, diagonals, flannel in small checks, plaids and so forth will make up stylishly in this way. The edges may be bound, stitched or plainly finished, as preferred.

A jaunty hat with a band of ribbon around the crown with short streamers falling at the back is appropriate to go with this costume.

Pattern No. 1092, *The Delineator,* **September 1886.**

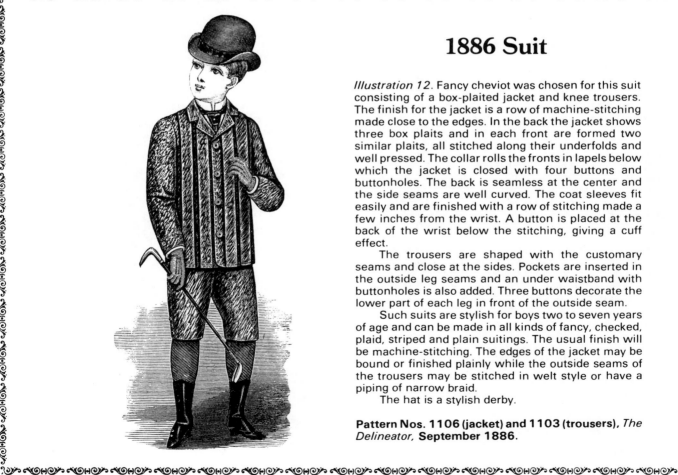

1886 Suit

Illustration 12. Fancy cheviot was chosen for this suit consisting of a box-plaited jacket and knee trousers. The finish for the jacket is a row of machine-stitching made close to the edges. In the back the jacket shows three box plaits and in each front are formed two similar plaits, all stitched along their underfolds and well pressed. The collar rolls the fronts in lapels below which the jacket is closed with four buttons and buttonholes. The back is seamless at the center and the side seams are well curved. The coat sleeves fit easily and are finished with a row of stitching made a few inches from the wrist. A button is placed at the back of the wrist below the stitching, giving a cuff effect.

The trousers are shaped with the customary seams and close at the sides. Pockets are inserted in the outside leg seams and an under waistband with buttonholes is also added. Three buttons decorate the lower part of each leg in front of the outside seam.

Such suits are stylish for boys two to seven years of age and can be made in all kinds of fancy, checked, plaid, striped and plain suitings. The usual finish will be machine-stitching. The edges of the jacket may be bound or finished plainly while the outside seams of the trousers may be stitched in welt style or have a piping of narrow braid.

The hat is a stylish derby.

Pattern Nos. 1106 (jacket) and 1103 (trousers), *The Delineator,* **September 1886.**

1886 Suit

Illustration 13. Very jaunty is this suit for a little man between three to ten years of age. The material illustrated in this instance is fancy suiting. The jacket has forward-turning plaits stitched in the back at each side of the center and in the front at each side of the closing; the closing is made in double-breasted style with buttonholes and buttons. The side seams are well curved. A belt stitched at all its edges is worn, its overlapping end being rounded and slipped through a strap fastened to the opposite end. The collar is in deep turnover style with rounding front corners. It is finished at its edges with a row of stitching. Pockets are inserted in the lower part of the fronts; the openings are finished with stitching and stayed at the ends with triangular ornaments done with silk twist. The coat sleeves fit easily and are plainly finished at their wrists.

The trousers are shaped by the usual seams and hip darts and have pockets in their outside seams. They close at the sides and have an under waistband with buttonholes in it so that the buttons supporting them will not be visible. The outside seams are stitched in welt style.

Suitings of all varieties including checks and hairlines will be used for suits of this style. Sometimes a leather belt will be worn. The trousers may be lined or not, as desired. The edges of the jacket may be bound or finished plainly.

The polo cap is made of the suit material and is a most fashionable chapeau for a small boy.

Pattern Nos. 1101 (jacket) and 1102 (trousers), *The Delineator,* **September 1886.**

1886 Costume

Illustration 14. A boy's costume made of plain cloth and decorated with braid and buttons.

Pattern No. 1092, *The Delineator,* **September 1886.**

1885

1885
Front View.

1885
Back View.

1888 Highland Costume

Illustration 15. Boy's highland costume including a matching hat.

Pattern No. 1885, *The Delineator,* **January 1888.**

1888 Suit

Illustration 16. This suit is developed in gray and black striped cheviot. It is appropriate for boys five to twelve years of age. The fronts of the coat turn back in small lapels; below the lapels the closing is made with four holes and buttons, the corners being rounded off stylishly below the lowest button. The side seams are placed well to the back. The center seam, which is symmetrically curved, is terminated a little above the lower edge at the top of narrow extensions that lap from the right side over the left in regular coat style. In each side of the front an opening is made for the customary side pocket; over it is arranged a broad welt. Higher up in the left side a shorter opening for a breast pocket is made. This is finished with a narrower welt. All the welts are stitched to the lower edges of the openings and have a row of stitching made below the seam and about their tops and ends. A high rolling collar meets the ends of the lapels in notches; its edges are finished with a row of stitching to correspond with the other edges of the coat. The sleeves have sufficient length for a hem finish at their wrists. Each has a row of stitching made in cuff outline not far above the hem, the cuff effect being completed by two buttons placed on the upper side in front of the outside seam.

The trousers extend a little below the knees and close with a fly. They may be worn with an underwaist or suspenders, as preferred, and the customary seams and hip darts are employed in shaping them. Two buttons are decoratively placed just in front of the outside seam near the bottom. Pockets are inserted in these seams near the belt.

Basket pattern diagonal, striped cashmere, silk mixed suitings and cheviots in either striped, checked or plaided varieties are available for such a suit. The edges may be completed plainly or finished with braid. Vegetable ivory, bone, horn, polished wood and braid-covered buttons are among the preferred varieties.

The hat is a natty derby shape.

Pattern Nos. 1987 (coat) and 1982 (trousers), *The Delineator,* **March 1888.**

1978
Front View.

1978
Back View.

1977
Front View.

1977
Back View.

1888 Costume

Illustration 17. Prune colored velvet and plaid wool goods showing a mixture of gold, prune and olive are associated in this instance. This stylish costume can be worn by boys from two to six years of age. A pleasing contrast is afforded by the choice of gold braid for the jacket trimming. The kilt is of the plaid goods and is laid in plaits that all turn in the same direction. It is joined to a sleeveless underwaist of silesia that is shaped by the customary underarm and shoulder seams and closes in front with buttonholes and flat buttons.

The jaunty little jacket is of velvet. Its front edges flare from the throat where they close with a hook and loop. Between the front edges is displayed a vest that is notched below its closing of buttonholes and smoked pearl buttons and is included with the side and shoulder seams at its back and shoulder edges respectively. The back of the jacket is seamless and falls a little below the waistline, its lower edge being unvaried in outline. Into the armseyes are sewn sleeves of the prevailing coat shape that are trimmed with braid in imitation of round cuffs. A round rolling collar outlined by two rows of braid is at the neck. The decorative items are completed by a tasteful arrangement of gold braid upon the front edges of the jacket, the braid being coiled in scrolls and curves.

Costumes uniting plaid fabrics with velvet, velveteen or corduroy are among the preferences of the season for small boys' wear. The adoption of a combination, however, is not essential to the successful development of the mode. A costume of dark blue cashmere designed for dressy wear is trimmed with black silk soutache and satin nail heads. Another, also for best wear, is of invisible green broadcloth with silver braid and buttons for trimming. A third illustrates the good effect of brown velvet with beige colored cloth, the jacket being of the velvet and the kilt of the cloth.

Pattern No. 1978, *The Delineator,* **March 1888.**

1888 Dress

Illustration 18. Little boy's dress.

Pattern No. 1977, *The Delineator,* **March 1888.**

1988
Front View.

1988
Back View.

1888 Cutaway Coat

Illustration 19. A fashionable boy's three-button cutaway coat.

Pattern No. 1988, *The Delineator,* **March 1888.**

1888 Suit

Illustration 20. A boy's suit worn smartly with a derby hat.

Pattern Nos. 1986 (jacket) and 1985 (trousers), *The Delineator,* **March 1888.**

1889 Costume

Illustration 21. The costume for boys two to six years old is here shown made of green smooth cloth, the trimming being supplied by fancy braid and buttons and a sash of cream white surah that has its ends fringed and knotted in tassel fashion. The kilt skirt is laid in broad plaits that turn toward the center of the back. The front ends of the skirt lap widely and are closed with buttonholes and fancy buttons, a row of buttons being ornamentally placed on the overlapping side. Back of the buttons at each side the skirt is decorated with a row of fancy braid. The skirt is joined to a sleeveless underwaist which is made of silesia and is shaped in the usual way.

The blouse is in the characteristic sailor fashion. The fronts are rolled by the collar, which they meet, and the edges are followed by braid. Vest portions are stitched flatly to the front. Below the collar four buttons are ornamentally placed along the line of stitching on each front. A sash, having its ends fringed and knotted in tassel style, is brought carelessly around the waist and tied in a sailor's knot at the left side. A patch pocket is stitched upon the left breast and a cuff is outlined on each sleeve by two rows of braid, a button being placed back of the wrist. A dainty sailor collar of white linen is worn at the neck and a ribbon bow is placed over its ends.

The costume may be developed in all kinds of flannel, serge, diagonal and so forth. It can be trimmed with soutache, metallic, gilt or any fancy braid. Anchors, chevrons, oars, stars and so forth may be embroidered on the collar and sleeves and buttons of similar design may be used. The sash may be made of the same material as the costume, the ends being knotted — or it may be omitted.

The jaunty Tam O'Shanter cap is of cloth to correspond with the costume; it is trimmed with a band of ribbon having a name embroidered in front.

Pattern No. 2873, *The Delineator,* **September 1889.**

2873
Front View.

2873
Back View.

1889 Costume

Illustration 22. In this instance the costume is made of navy blue French flannel trimmed with tan braid and buttons. This costume is developed differently in *Illustration 21.*

Pattern No. 2873, *The Delineator,* **September 1889.**

1889 Overcoat

Illustration 23. The overcoat, stylish for boys four to fifteen years of age, is shown made of smooth-faced overcoating with velvet for the collar. The edges are finished with machine-stitching and the cape is lined with silk. The adjustment is performed by side-back gores and a well-curved center seam which terminates above coat laps. To the front edge of each front is joined a lapel which reaches to the waistline. The body is closed with buttons and buttonholes in double-breasted fashion. Each front is deepened by an added skirt that is joined to the back with which it forms an underfolded, forward-turning plait. The cape, which reaches almost to the waistline, is fitted smoothly over the shoulders by darts. At the neck is a rolling collar that flares at the throat. Two rows of stitching outline a cuff upon each close-fitting sleeve. In the left breast is inserted a pocket that is finished with a welt.

All sorts of coatings may be used for a garment of this kind, melton, diagonal, corkscrew, kersey and so forth being most frequently chosen. For cold weather the cape may be made of fur or astrakhan which will add much to the stylish effect of the garment. When diagonal or other dressy goods are made up, the edges will be bound with narrow silk or silk and mohair braid. A lining of serge, silk or Italian is generally added to a coat of this kind; flannel is substituted when extra warmth is desired. An especially dressy garment may be made of smooth-faced navy blue cloth, the collar and wrists being richly trimmed with beaver fur.

The hat is a stylish derby.

Pattern No. 2875, *The Delineator,* **September 1889.**

Front View.

Front View.

Back View.

Back View.

1889 Frock Overcoat

Illustration 24. The boy's frock overcoat is here made of light overcoating and the edges are followed by machine-stitching. The fronts are closed in double-breasted fashion. To the front edge of each front a lapel is sewn. The coat is lengthened at the front and at each side by a skirt, the back edge of which is joined to the front edge of the back, the fullness being underfolded to form a forward-turning plait that is marked at the top with a button. The adjustment is performed by center, side and side-back seams, the first being terminated above coat laps. A pocket is inserted in the left breast and finished with a welt. The cape, which reaches nearly to the waistline and flares at the front, is fitted smoothly over each shoulder by a dart. At the neck is a rolling collar that also flares at the throat. Upon each of the comfortable coat sleeves a cuff is outlined with machine-stitching. This overcoat is suitable for boys four to fifteen years old.

Melton, kersey, diagonal, corkscrew and mixed, plain, striped and checked overcoating will make up handsomely by the mode. The finish may be plain, or for cold weather wear, the cuffs and collar may be of fur. Astrakhan may be used for trimming, the cape being frequently made of it with stylish effect. A lining of serge, Italian or silk is generally used but when extra warmth is desired, flannel is substituted.

Pattern No. 2875, *The Delineator,* **September 1889.**

1889 Coat

Illustration 25. This coat to be worn by boys five to fifteen years old is made of fancy suiting and trimmed with buttons, a line of machine-stitching following all the edges and outlining cuffs upon the sleeves. The fronts close on the breast with three buttons. Below the closing they are rounded away with a decided flare while above the closing they are reversed by a rolling collar that meets the lapels in notches. The center seam is continued to the lower edge. The side seams are left open a short distance from the bottom, narrow extensions being allowed on the back edges of the fronts. The side pockets are finished with flaps having rounding lower front corners and the left breast pocket is finished with a welt. The edges of the cash pocket are followed with machine-stitching. The outside seam of each of the closely fitting sleeves is discontinued at the top of a narrow extension allowed on the underside. A button is placed back of the wrist.

All seasonable suitings and coatings may be developed by the mode. The finish may be plain or a line of machine-stitching may be made close to the edge. Braid binding forms an admired finish on plain or twilled cloth. Long or knee trousers and a vest may be worn with the coat which may be cut from different material if desired.

Pattern No. 2878, *The Delineator,* **September 1889.**

1889 Reefer Suit

Illustration 26. Boy's reefer suit developed here in cashmere and trimmed with brass buttons and gilt embroidery.

Pattern Nos. 2876 (jacket) and 2580 (trousers), *The Delineator,* **September 1889.**

2934
Front View.

2934
Back View.

1889 Costume

Illustration 28. The costume illustrated is made of velvet and striped and plain cloth, braid being used for trim. It can be seen made up differently in *Illustration 27.*

Pattern No. 2934, *The Delineator,* **November 1889.**

1889 Costume

Illustration 27. This costume for boys between two and six years of age, is made of plaid serge, black velvet and surah and trimmed with braid. The skirt is kilt plaited except for a short distance at the front where it is given the effect of a broad box plait. The lower edge is hemmed. The top of the skirt is finished with a belt beneath which is placed a waistband with buttonholes worked in it.

The waist is fitted by underarm and shoulder seams. The fronts are turned under for hems and closed with buttons and buttonholes. The neck and armseye edges are finished with underfacings and a linen collar shows prettily above the jacket.

The jacket is adjusted stylishly to the figure by a well-curved center and side seams, the fronts suggesting the Spanish style. At the neck is a rolling collar with rounding ends. Cuffs are outlined on the coat sleeves with braid; a row of braid also follows the outline of the collar and jacket. A sash of surah with fringed ends is adjusted about the top of the skirt and loosely knotted a little to the left side.

Combinations will develop stylishly in this way and flannel, cheviot, lady's cloth, diagonal and many other dress fabrics unite well with velvet or corduroy. If velvet is too dressy for everyday wear, plain wool goods may be used, a contrasting color being generally preferred. Gilt, metallic, soutache or fancy woolen braid may be used for trimming. The sash may be made of the plain material. If desired, rows of buttons may be placed on the plain portion of the skirt or it may be crossed with braid.

The stylish jockey cap is of velvet, the top decorated with a button.

Pattern No. 2934, *The Delineator,* **November 1889.**

8993
Front View.

8993
Back View.

1889 Eton Jacket

Illustration 29. The Eton jacket is always admired and this season is especially popular for boys seven to fifteen years of age. Cloth of a quality adapted to school wear is illustrated in this instance, the finish being plain. The fronts turn back in long lapels at their upper portions. Below the lapels they are provided with three buttonholes and buttons for closing. Side backs curving into the armseyes and a center seam that inclines more toward the waistline than is common in boys' garments fit the back in a shapely manner. The jacket extends but a little below the waistline; its lower edge is decidely, though not deeply, pointed at the center of the back and front, the outline curving upward proportionately over the hips. A rolling collar with a seam at the center where it is quite narrow meets the lapels in notches. The sleeves have the seams peculiar to the coat shape and show high curves at their tops which left them over the shoulders in the most comfortable manner. Enough extra length is allowed for a hem at the lower edge of each sleeve. A row of machine-stitching holds the hem in position.

Eton jackets may be made of any fabric adapted to boys' wear such as tricot, diagonal, hair-line suitings and any variety of striped, plaid or mixed cloths are adaptable to the fashion but plain cloth is almost universally chosen. The outline of the garment is so attractive that the simplest finish is in better taste, though binds of braid are always good form. Careful pressing is always necessary to produce a good effect.

Pattern No. 8993, *The Delineator,* **December 1889.**

1890 Costume

Illustration 30. This costume to be worn by boys from two to six years of age is pictured developed in plaid wool goods and plain dark and light serge with nail-head buttons and braid forming the decoration. The stylish little skirt is supported by a sleeveless waist of lining that is shaped by underarm and shoulder seams and closed at the center of the back. It falls in kilt plaits turning toward the center at each side of the back and in wide box plaits at the front and sides.

The front and back of the blouse are united by underarm and shoulder seams and finished at the lower edge with a belt, below which the fullness droops in characteristic blouse fashion. At the neck is a deep sailor collar that is turned from a neckband and outlined near its free edges by a row of machine-stitching. The shirt-sleeves are each gathered at the wrist to a narrow wristband from which is upturned a deep round cuff outlined at its upper edge by a row of stitching.

The jaunty little jacket worn over the blouse is fitted by underarm and shoulder seams; the fronts flare from the neck to fall in square outline at each side of the closing of the blouse. The lower outline is varied by discontinuing the underarm seams for a short distance from the edge and notching the back correspondingly at the center. All the free edges of the back and fronts are bound with braid and a row of nail-head buttons is placed along each edge of the notch and each free edge of the underarm seams. The jacket is passed under the collar of the blouse and the cuffs of the blouse sleeves are turned over the coat sleeves of the jacket. A Turkish sash is tied about the waist to fall in ends at the left of the center in front.

The cap is made of dark cloth. It has a circular crown and its sides, which are seamed together at the center of the front and back, are joined to the crown and to a narrow band that fits the head and is covered by a ribbon tied to fall in ends at the center of the back.

Combinations of dark velvets with wash silks and plain or fancy woolens will develop handsomely in a costume of this description. The design is also nicely adapted to gingham, seersucker, piqué, cambric, flannel and other washable textures. The jacket may be prettily decorated with fancy braids and the sailor collar and the cuffs with embroidered emblems or braiding. Any dark cloth or flannel may be chosen for the sailor cap.

Pattern Nos. 3286 (suit) and 3033 (cap), *The Delineator,* **June 1890.**

1890 Costume

Illustration 31. This costume, first shown in *Illustration 30*, is here made of velvet, pongee and surah silks and cashmere, with tassels and fancy edging and insertion matching the pongee silk for decoration. The free edges of the collar and cuffs and the over-lapping edge of the closing of the blouse are decorated with frills of edging headed with bands of insertion. The ends of the surah sash are gathered and tipped with tassels.

The cap, which matches the jacket, is formed of six sections that are curved outward at their side edges and pointed at the top. The sections are seamed together at their curved edges so that the points meet at the center and a visor stiffened by an interlining of canvas is joined to the front of the cap.

Plain, fancy striped or spotted flannels or cloth may be selected for the cap. Its sections will sometimes be of contrasting colors or alternately of plain and fancy material.

Pattern Nos. 3286 (suit) and 3166 (cap), *The Delineator,* **June 1890.**

3286
Front View.

3286
Back View.

1890 Costume

Illustration 32. This is the same costume as shown in *Illustrations 30* and *31*. Piqué, lawn, all-over embroidery and surah are combined in the costume in the present instance.

Pattern No. 3286, *The Delineator,* **June 1890.**

1890 Dress

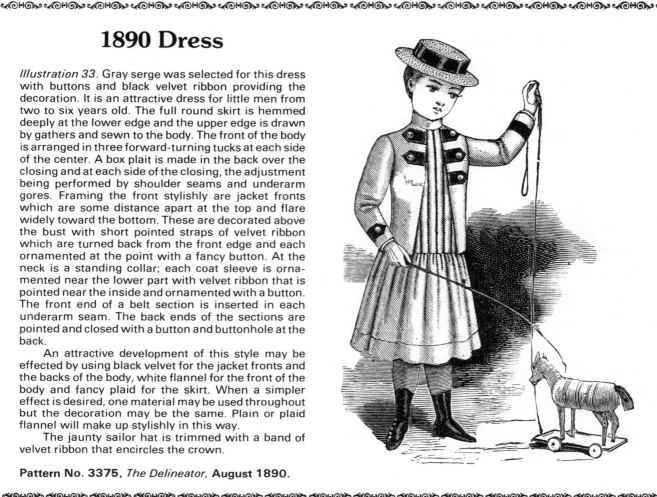

Illustration 33. Gray serge was selected for this dress with buttons and black velvet ribbon providing the decoration. It is an attractive dress for little men from two to six years old. The full round skirt is hemmed deeply at the lower edge and the upper edge is drawn by gathers and sewn to the body. The front of the body is arranged in three forward-turning tucks at each side of the center. A box plait is made in the back over the closing and at each side of the closing, the adjustment being performed by shoulder seams and underarm gores. Framing the front stylishly are jacket fronts which are some distance apart at the top and flare widely toward the bottom. These are decorated above the bust with short pointed straps of velvet ribbon which are turned back from the front edge and each ornamented at the point with a fancy button. At the neck is a standing collar; each coat sleeve is ornamented near the lower part with velvet ribbon that is pointed near the inside and ornamented with a button. The front end of a belt section is inserted in each underarm seam. The back ends of the sections are pointed and closed with a button and buttonhole at the back.

An attractive development of this style may be effected by using black velvet for the jacket fronts and the backs of the body, white flannel for the front of the body and fancy plaid for the skirt. When a simpler effect is desired, one material may be used throughout but the decoration may be the same. Plain or plaid flannel will make up stylishly in this way.

The jaunty sailor hat is trimmed with a band of velvet ribbon that encircles the crown.

Pattern No. 3375, *The Delineator,* **August 1890.**

3375
Front View.

3375
Back View.

1890 Dress

Illustration 34. The dress, the same pattern as shown in *Illustration 33*, is developed in plaid gingham and decorated with narrow Hamburg embroidered edging.

Pattern No. 3375, *The Delineator,* **August 1890.**

1891 Costume

Illustration 35. This costume for boys two to seven years old is made of blue serge and velvet. The skirt is arranged in kilt plaits that turn from a broad box plait at the center of the front, the lower part of the box plait being ornamented at each side with a row of buttons and simulated buttonholes. The skirt is joined to the sleeveless body which is adjusted by shoulder seams and closed at the back with buttons and buttonholes.

The fronts of the jacket are folded over to form revers to the lower edge, the revers being decorated with buttons and simulated buttonholes. At the back and sides the seams of the jacket are discontinued a short distance from the lower edge to form square tabs. The coat sleeves are trimmed at their wrists with buttons and simulated buttonholes; the lower edges are finished with machine-stitching. Similar stitching ornaments the edge of the deep sailor collar which falls square at the back. A spotted silk scarf is worn. All the remaining edges of the jacket and the lower edge of the skirt are finished with a row of stitching.

Plain, plaid, striped and mixed suitings may be developed in a costume of this kind. If a combination of fabrics be not desired, a single material may be employed throughout. For decoration silk or mohair braid or machine-stitching will usually be applied.

The hat is a sailor shape of fine dark straw.

Pattern No. 3782, *The Delineator,* **March 1891.**

1891 Suit

Illustration 36. Striped and two shades of plain jersey cloth are here united in a suit for boys four to sixteen years old. The shirt is shaped by shoulder and underarm seams; the front is cut away in V shape to accommodate a shield which is permanently sewn at the right side and fastened invisibly beneath the left side. The sailor collar falls in regulation style at the back; its tapering ends extend to the end of the V where a bow of ribbon is ornamentally applied. The sleeves have each but one seam and the wrists are plainly completed.

The trousers extend a trifle below the knee and are shaped by the customary seams along the inside and outside of the leg and at the center of the front and back. They close with a fly and pockets are inserted in the side seams. Eiderdown flannel, jersey flannel, silk jersey webbing and other elastic fabrics may be employed in developing the shirt. For the trousers similar material or corkscrew, diagonal, serge or any other plain or fancy suiting may be used. Machine-stitching or braid may be used for a completion or a perfectly plain finish may be adopted.

The cap is of the darker jersey cloth.

Pattern Nos. 3778 (shirt) and 3783 (trousers), *The Delineator,* **March 1891.**

3741

Front View.

3741

Back View.

1891 Child's Coat

Illustration 37. Child's coat.

Pattern No. 3741, *The Delineator,* **March 1891.**

3788

Front View.

3788

Back View.

1891 Dress

Illustration 39. The dress is here developed in plain and plaid wool goods. It is shown differently in *Illustration 38.*

Pattern No. 3788, *The Delineator,* **April 1891.**

1891 Dress

Illustration 38. Figured white piqué is the material represented in this dress for boys two to six years of age. The skirt is arranged in well-pressed kilt plaits that all turn in the same direction and is joined to the body which is adjusted by shoulder and side seams and closed at the front with buttons and buttonholes. At each side of the closing are two forward-turning tucks; two backward-turning tucks are made at each side of the center of the back. The coat sleeves are ornamented at the wrists with embroidered edging, the scalloped edge of which turns upward. A dainty frill of similar edging droops prettily from the edge of the rolling collar. The waist is encircled by a belt that closes at the front with buttons and buttonholes.

The cap is made of velvet. The crown is composed of six pointed sections stiffened with canvas and a peak also stiffened with canvas is joined to the front of the crown. A velvet button is placed on the crown at the top. The cap is lined throughout with silk.

The dress will develop stylishly in all sorts of seasonable woolens such as fancy or plaid suitings, flannel, serge and striped, checked, mottled or shot cheviots. Combinations of plain and plaid goods may be effected by the mode with pleasing results; velvet is stylish for combining with all textures. Silk, worsted or other braids, bias bands, stitching and so forth may be employed for trimming. The belt may match the dress in material and be closed with a buckle, slide or strap, or it may be of leather or metal as preferred. The cap may match or contrast with the dress in texture or color. The front may be appropriately decorated with a strap secured at each end with an ornamental button.

Pattern Nos. 3788 (dress) and 3166 (cap), *The Delineator,* **April 1891.**

1891 Sailor Suit

Illustration 40. This sailor suit consists of a blouse and trousers, appropriate for boys four to twelve years old. It is developed in a combination of dark blue and white flannel with white braid for decoration. The trousers are shaped by the usual leg seams and by a seam at the center of the front and back. The fronts are made with a fall bearer, the closing being performed in regulation style at the sides and across the front with buttonholes and buttons. A pocket is inserted in the right back. A waistband completes the top.

The blouse is made upon a short lining; the lower edge is gathered, the fullness drooping in the usual way below the belt. The neck is cut in low, pointed outline to reveal a shield attached to the lining with buttons and buttonholes. The shield is ornamented with crosswise rows of white braid and the fronts are closed with a white lacing cord. The ends of the cord are tied in a bow below the ends of the white sailor collar which falls deep and square at the back. The sleeves are in full shirt-sleeve style and are finished at the wrists with cuffs.

The cap is known as the "Commodore" and is here illustrated made of blue cloth. It has a circular crown to the edge of which the side is joined. The side is in four sections and both it and the crown are lined with silk. The band joins the lower edge of the side; the visor is stiffened with cardboard or canvas.

Flannel, silk jersey cloth and numerous woolens may be used for sailor suits with very satisfactory results. For little boys' summer suits, piqué, percale and seersucker will be admired. The cap may be made of blue or white cloth, flannel or piqué.

Pattern Nos. 4032 (sailor suit) and 3267 (cap), *The Delineator,* **September 1891.**

1891 Overcoat

Illustration 41. Fancy seven-year-old overcoating was employed for this stylish overcoat for two to seven-year-old boys. Velvet was used for the collar. The fronts, which are rendered smooth at the sides by darts, lap widely and close in double-breasted fashion with large buttons and buttonholes. The back is nicely conformed to the figure by side-back seams and a center seam that terminates above stylish coat laps. Coat plaits arranged in the side-back seams complete the jaunty effect. The coat sleeves are comfortably wide and are finished at the wrists with machine-stitching applied at deep cuff depth from the edge. The square-cornered pocket laps concealing the openings to side pockets are finished with similar stitching. The rolling collar is made of velvet and beneath it the military cape is attached by means of buttons and buttonholes or hooks and eyes. The military cape is adjusted on the shoulders by darts and falls with easy fullness to the regulation depth. A pretty lining of farmer satin or fancy serge may be added if desired.

The cap is made of velvet. Six triangular sections are united to form the crown; a peak stiffened with canvas is joined to the front of the crown. A button ornaments the top.

Overcoats of kersey, melton, beaver, diagonal and tweed are very stylish for little boys' wear over kilt costumes. Any of the above mentioned fabrics will develop attractively by the mode with machine-stitching or braid for a finish. The cap may be made of the same kind of material as the overcoat or of flannel, tennis cloth and so forth and is appropriate for athletic sports of all kinds.

Pattern Nos. 4026 (overcoat) and 3166 (cap), *The Delineator,* **September 1891.**

1891 Costume

Illustration 42. The costume for two to six-year-old boys is pictured made of plaid wool goods and plain velvet with gilt cord supplying effective decoration. The skirt, which is cut bias, is plain at the center of the front while the sides and back are arranged in kilt plaits that all turn toward the back. The skirt is joined by means of buttons and buttonholes made in the waistband to the sleeveless body. The waistband is covered by a belt made of the plaid material. The body is shaped by shoulder and underarm seams and is partially revealed between the rounding edges of the velvet jacket fronts. Pocket openings in the fronts are finished with machine-stitching.

The jacket is of stylish length and is gracefully curved to the figure at the back and side back seams. The edge of the jacket is prettily ornamented with gilt cord fancifully applied; the coat sleeves are each decorated at cuff depth from the edge with two rows of similar cord. The rolling collar is trimmed to correspond.

The jaunty cloth polo cap has a circular crown to the edge of which the side is sewn. The cap is lined throughout with silk.

The costume may be developed in any fashionable variety of cloth, serge, fancy, plaid and plain flannel and so forth. Velvet will be used for the jacket with most attractive results, but, if preferred, a single wool fabric may be employed for the entire costume. The cap may be of cloth, velvet or serge and may match or prettily contrast with the costume.

Pattern Nos. 4034 (costume) and 3167 (cap), *The Delineator,* **September 1891.**

4031
Front View.

4031
Back View.

1891 Overcoat

Illustration 43. Boy's long overcoat with military cape.

Pattern No. 4031, *The Delineator,* **September 1891.**

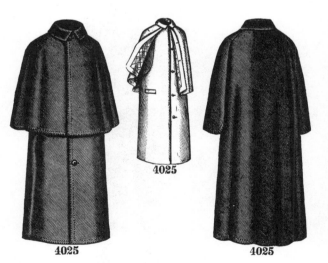

4025
Front View.

4025

4025
Back View.

1891 Inverness Overcoat

Illustration 44. Boy's inverness overcoat in this instance made of fine diagonal corkscrew and finished with machine-stitching.

Pattern No. 4025, *The Delineator,* **September 1891.**

1892 Suit

1892 Suits

Illustrations 45 and 46. Two boys' suits from Butterick advertisements.

The Delineator, **circa 1892.**

Illustration 47. Checked cheviot was used for this suit and it was finished with machine-stitching. The trousers are shaped by the customary leg seams and extend a little below the knees; the closing is made in a fly. Side pockets are inserted, the top finished with a waistband. The suit can be worn by boys five to sixteen years old.

The fronts of the vest are closed with five holes and buttons and are shaped to accommodate a notched collar that rolls high at the back. The back is curved to the figure by a center seam below which it is deeply notched. The curved side seams are terminated a little above the lower edge. The customary straps cross the back and a buckle regulates the adjustment. The openings to side pockets and breast pockets are finished with welts. All the edges are followed with a row of machine-stitching. Four to sixteen year old boys can wear this vest.

The sack coat is closed with one hole and button below which its front edges are rounded in cutaway fashion. Shoulder and underarm seams perform the adjustment. The fronts are reversed by a rolling collar to form lapels. The coat sleeves are of comfortable width and plainly completed. Two side pockets, a left breast pocket and a change pocket are applied to the fronts in patch style and are finished with machine-stitching. Machine-stitching also follows all the loose edges of the coat.

Cheviot and mixed, shot, striped, checked and fancy suitings will make up fashionably in this way. The edges of the coat and vest may be bound with braid. Round cuffs may be outlined on the sleeves with machine-stitching but a plain completion is always appropriate.

The hat is a derby of fine felt.

Pattern Nos. 4391 (sack coat), 4394 (vest) and 4395 (trousers), *The Delineator,* **March 1892.**

1892 Costume

Illustration 48. This costume for two to seven-year-old boys is illustrated made of shot cloth. The jacket fronts flare gradually from the neck to disclose a vest which is closed at the center with buttons and buttonholes and shapes a notch below the closing. The fronts are adjusted by underarm darts in which the back edges of the vest are included. The back is curved to the form by the usual center and side seams which are discontinued to form the back in rounding tabs below the waistline. The coat sleeves are of comfortable width and at the neck is a rolling collar. The jacket fronts are decorated with a fanciful arrangement of black braid. Pocket laps concealing the openings to side pockets are each trimmed with three rows of braid. The vest is provided with side pockets and its front and lower edges are bound with braid. The skirt is arranged in uniform kilt plaits and is attached by means of buttons and buttonholes to a shirtwaist, the sleeveless body provided by the pattern being here omitted.

The shirtwaist is made of fine white linen lawn. Three forward-turning plaits are laid at each side of the closing which is made at the center of the front. Three backward-turning plaits appear at each side of the center. A box plait is arranged over the closing, its edges being decorated with box-plaited frills of doubled material. The shirtwaist is furnished with a waistband upon which buttons are sewn for the attachment of the skirt. The shirt-sleeves are finished with deep round cuffs which are trimmed with box-plait frills and are rolled over the sleeves of the jacket. The collar rolls deeply over the jacket and is decorated to correspond with the cuffs. A stylish Windsor scarf is worn.

The cap is made of dark blue cloth. It consists of two sections — a band that fits the head closely and a crown which joins the band and is widened and shaped by a seam at the center of the front and back and a seam at each side to present the regulation mortarboard shape. A tassel droops prettily at the side.

All kinds of suitings in mottled, shot, checked and striped effects will make up well in a costume of this description. The shirtwaist may be of plain or figured percale, linen, cambric or other washable material. The cap will usually be of cloth in dark blue, tan or black.

Pattern Nos. 4396 (suit), 4399 (shirtwaist) and 4393 (cap), *The Delineator,* **March 1892.**

1892 Dress

Illustration 49. This dress is made of white piqué, has a kilt-plaited skirt joined to a waist that has sack fronts and a French back and extends over the hips. The closing is made at the front, and the joining of the skirt and body is concealed by a wide, curved belt, the pointed ends of which are closed at the front with buttons and buttonholes. A standing collar is at the neck. The sleeves are in coat sleeve shape. It can be worn by little boys from two to five years of age.

The jacket is made of velvet and is closed in double-breasted style to the throat, the front edges below the closing being cut away to produce a notched effect. The loose fronts are curved to the figure at the sides by underarm darts; the back is shaped by a curving center seam. The fronts and back are joined in curving side seams which, with the center seam, are discontinued some distance above the lower edge to form tabs at the back. The wrists of the shapely coat sleeves are trimmed with round cuffs simulated with flat braid. Similar braid edges the sailor collar which falls square at the back and flares widely at the throat. The opening to a breast pocket inserted in the left front is bound with braid. Pocket laps which cover the openings to side pockets are finished to correspond. The jacket is appropriate for lads two to seven years old.

The cap is made of dark blue cloth and is described in *Illustration 48*.

Smart little suits of this kind may be developed in materials suitable for both dressy and general wear. Cloths and suitings will make up as satisfactorily as piqué in a dress of this kind and the jacket may be of checked, plaid, striped or fancy cloth, cheviot, serge, homespun, diagonal and so forth. The cap may match or contrast with the remainder of the suit.

Pattern Nos. 2570 (dress), 4401 (jacket) and 4393 (cap), *The Delineator*, **March 1892.**

1892 Suit

Illustration 50. Mixed cheviot was used in this suit for boys three to sixteen years old.

Machine-stitching provides a neat finish. The trousers reach a trifle below the knees and are shaped by the usual seams and the closing is made in a fly. A pocket is inserted at each side and the top is provided with a waistband.

The back of the jacket-blouse is curved to the figure by a center seam at each side of which a backward-turning plait it made and stitched to position. A forward-turning plait is similarly stitched in each front. The closing is made in double-breasted style. The fronts are reversed at the top to form lapels that meet the rolling collar in notches. Straps cross the back at the waistline and are buttoned over the center seam. All of the edges of the blouse are followed by a single row of machine-stitching and two rows of stitching outline a round cuff upon each of the coat sleeves which are of comfortable width, two buttons being also placed at the back of the wrist.

The jaunty polo cap has a circular crown to the edge of which is sewn the side. The cap is lined with silk.

The suit may be developed in any fashionable variety of suiting such as cheviot, corkscrew, diagonal, tricot, corduroy and so forth. Machine-stitching or braid will contribute a neat finish. The cap may be of the same or of a contrasting material.

Pattern Nos. 4392 (jacket-blouse), 4395 (trousers) and 3167 (cap), *The Delineator*, **March 1892.**

1892 Fauntleroy Suit

Illustration 51. Black velvet, white silk and Irish point embroidery are united in this Fauntleroy costume. Little boys from two to seven years of age will wear this suit. The trousers extend a trifle below the knee and are shaped by darts and the customary leg seams; the closing is made at the sides. The trousers are attached with buttons and buttonholes to a shirtwaist which is shaped by shoulder and underarm seams. It is closed at the front with buttons and buttonholes, a box plait being arranged over the closing. The shirt-sleeves are joined to wristbands and finished with deep round cuffs of Irish point embroidery. The cuffs and the sailor collar, which is of similar embroidery and mounted on a band, roll prettily over the sleeves and neck of the jacket.

The fronts of the jacket are closed at the center with buttons and buttonholes; the back is curved to the figure by a center seam. The fronts and back are joined in shoulder and side seams, the latter seams being curved to define the figure becomingly. A tassel-tipped silk sash encircles the waist and is prettily knotted at the left side.

The cap is made of black velvet. Six triangular sections are united to form the crown; a peak stiffened with canvas is joined to the front of the crown and a button ornaments the top.

Suits of this kind are among the most popular styles for little boys and cloth, flannel, serge and diagonal are appropriately used for them. For general wear plain or mixed cheviot will be stylish and comfortable. The cap may match or contrast with the costume it accompanies.

Pattern Nos. 4716 (costume) and 3166 (cap), *The Delineator,* **September 1892.**

4716
Front View.

4716
Back View.

1892 Fauntleroy Suit

Illustration 52. The stylish costume previously pictured in *Illustration 51* is presently made of dark blue velvet, white silk, cambric and all-over embroidery.

Pattern No. 4716, *The Delineator,* **September 1892.**

1892 Russian Suit

Illustration 53. A little boy's Russian suit for two to seven year olds is made up in navy blue flannel. The trousers are in knickerbocker style and are shaped by the usual seams, the closing being made at the sides. The lower edges of the trousers are turned under for hems in which elastics are inserted to draw the garment closely to the legs, the fullness drooping in regulation fashion.

The Russian blouse reaches nearly to the knee and is seamless at the back. Its left front laps to the right shoulder seam and is disposed with pretty fullness by gathers at the neck. The right front is plain and narrow; the closing is made invisibly at the right side. The waist is encircled by a leather belt. The front edge of the overlapping front is trimmed with fancy braid; similar braid covers the neck band. The full shirt-sleeves are gathered at the top and bottom and are finished with wristbands which are trimmed with braid and closed at the back of the arms with buttons and buttonholes.

The jaunty cloth polo cap has a circular crown to the edge of which the side is sewn. The cap is lined throughout with silk.

The suit may be developed in any seasonable variety of serge, flannel, cloth or fancy, checked, plaid or striped suiting. The cap may be of cloth or serge and may match or prettily contrast with the suit.

Pattern Nos. 4717 (suit) and 3167 (cap), *The Delineator,* **September 1892.**

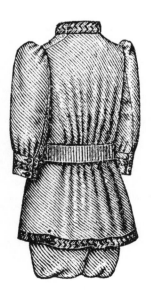

1892 Russian Suit

Illustration 54. The Russian suit is illustrated made of dark blue serge and trimmed with fancy braid. It is developed differently in *Illustration 53.*

Pattern No. 4717, *The Delineator,* **September 1892.**

Front View.   Back View.

1892 Sailor Blouse Costume

Illustration 55. The costume to be worn by boys two to seven years old is here represented developed in blue and white serge. The skirt is arranged in a broad box plait at the center of the front and at the back and sides in well-pressed kilt plaits that turn toward the front. The lower edge of the skirt is finished with a hem. The top is joined to a sleeveless body which is shaped by shoulder and underarm seams and closed at the back with buttons and buttonholes.

The usual shaping seams enter into the adjustment of the blouse. It is closed at the center of the front with buttons and buttonholes through a box plait made in the left front. The lower edge is hemmed for a casing in which an elastic is run. The garment droops with the customary fullness over the skirt. The fronts are cut away to disclose a facing of white cloth applied to the front of the sleeveless body and short V-shaped facings are arranged upon the backs of the body. The sailor collar falls deep and square at the back. Its long tapering ends are joined to the cutaway edges of the fronts and upon the facing revealed between is an embroidered star. The collar is trimmed with fancy braid. The cuffs, which finish the full shirt-sleeves, are decorated to correspond. A patch pocket having a pointed lap is applied to the left side of the blouse. It is trimmed with two rows of fancy braid and holds a whistle which is attached to a lanyard worn about the neck.

Blue and white striped flannel, serge and cloth are fashionable for costumes of this kind. There are numerous cotton fabrics that may be satisfactorily used such as seersucker, percale and gingham. Braid, embroidered nautical emblems or machine-stitching will contribute tasteful garniture, although a plain completion will be in perfect taste.

The hat is a blue sailor banded with white ribbon.

Pattern No. 4715, *The Delineator,* **September 1892.**

4715
Front View.

4715
*Front View
without
Blouse.*

4715
*Back View
without
Blouse.*

4715
Back View.

1892 Sailor Blouse Costume

Illustration 56. Blue and white striped flannel and plain blue flannel are united in this blouse costume with very stylish effect, narrow white braid, machine-stitching and an embroidered anchor providing the decoration. This costume is also shown in *Illustration 55.*

Pattern No. 4715, *The Delineator,* **September 1892.**

1892 Suit

1892 Suit

Illustration 57. Another suit for two to seven year olds is developed in dark cheviot and light cloth and finished with machine-stitching. The skirt, which is made of cheviot, is arranged in kilt plaits all round and is finished at the top with a waistband in which are made buttonholes that pass over buttons sewn to the shirt-waist.

The overcoat extends to a little below the waist and has a uniform lower outline. The fronts are reversed at the top in small lapels by a rolling collar which meets the lapels in notches. Below the lapels the closing is made in a fly. The center and side seams are well curved to the form, the side seams being discontinued a short distance from the lower edge. The sleeves are of comfortable width. Each wrist is finished with several rows of machine-stitching. Pocket laps cover the openings to side pockets in the fronts and to a breast pocket in the left front. Their upper edges are neatly finished with three close rows of machine-stitching. All the loose edges of the garment are finished with a double row of machine-stitching. The body seams of the coat and the outside seams of the sleeves are strapped; a strap is stylishly applied a little distance back of the front edge of the left front.

The jaunty cap is made of the same kind of material as the overcoat. The circular crown is interlined with one or two thicknesses of canvas or crinoline and is joined to the side. The band is sewn to the loose edge of the side and is joined in a seam at the center of the back beneath ribbon ends.

Striped, plaid, mixed, checked and plain cloths will make up satisfactorily in this way. For general wear the finish will usually be plain. The cap may be made of cloth, corduroy or velvet or, if preferred, material like that in the top coat may be used.

Pattern Nos. 4707 (overcoat) and 4718 (Kiltskirt) 4718, *The Delineator,* **September 1892.**

Illustration 58. Light mixed cheviot and dark velvet are stylishly united in this costume fashionable for two to seven-year-old boys. The skirt is arranged in kilt plaits that all turn in the same direction. A hem finishes the lower edge. The top is completed with a belt and with an under waistband in which buttonholes are made to provide a means of attachment to the sleeveless body that is shaped by shoulder and underarm seams and closed at the front with buttons and buttonholes.

The jacket fronts meet at the throat and are rounded off toward the back which has a curving center seam that defines the figure nicely. The fronts join the backs in curved side seams. The front and lower edges of the jacket are trimmed with silk cord. The rolling collar is decorated to correspond; similar cord is applied to the shapely coat sleeves in round cuff outline. Two silk ornaments are added to each sleeve at the wrist. Similar ornaments trim the jacket fronts effectively.

The cap is in Tam O'Shanter or sailor style and is made of dark velvet. The side has a seam at the center of the front and back and is sewn to the edge of the circular crown. The word "Atlantic" appears on a ribbon covering the band which is sewn to the side and gives the cap a truly nautical air.

Plain, plaid, checked and striped suitings will develop becoming costumes of this kind. Braid or machine-stitching may supply the decoration. The cap may be made of cloth, corduroy or velvet or, if preferred, it may match the suit it accompanies. A stylish suit may be made of Scotch plaid and dark green velvet, the latter forming the jacket and cap.

Pattern Nos. 4708 (costume) and 3033 (cap), *The Delineator,* **September 1892.**

1892 Costume

Illustration 59. A variation of the little boy's suit in *Illustration 58.*

Pattern 4708, *The Delineator,* **September 1892.**

4708 **4708**

Front View. *Back View.*

1892 Overcoat

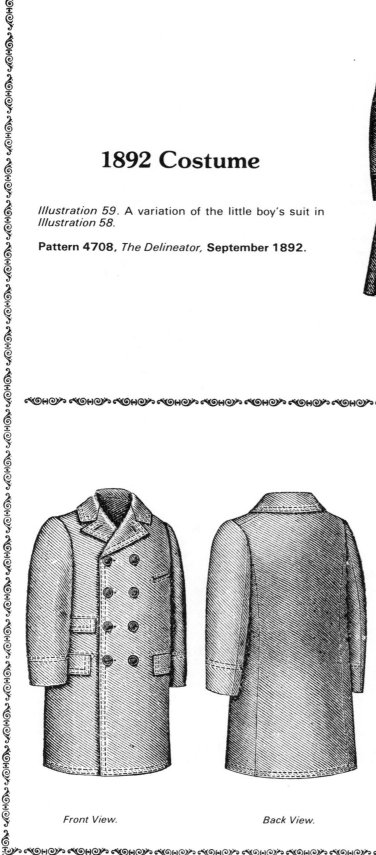

Illustration 60. A boy's overcoat for which a fine quality of melton was selected in this instance. Machine-stitching provides a stylish finish. The fronts lap widely and close in double-breasted fashion with buttons and buttonholes. They are reversed in lapels by a rolling collar that meets the lapels in notches; a buttonhole is worked in each lapel. The back is seamless at the center while the side seams are curved well to the figure. The coat sleeves are comfortably wide and are each finished with two rows of machine-stitching. Pocket laps cover the openings to side pockets in the fronts and to a change pocket in the right front. All edges of the overcoat are followed with a double row of machine-stitching.

All fashionable varieties of overcoating may be made up in this way, chevron, chinchilla, tweed, kersey, cloth and diagonal being among the most suitable. If machine-stitching be undesirable, a plain completion may be adopted. A comfortable and stylish overcoat may be made by the mode of mixed gray smooth cloth and lined with gray satin.

Pattern No. 4709, *The Delineator,* **September 1892.**

Front View. *Back View.*

1893 Apron

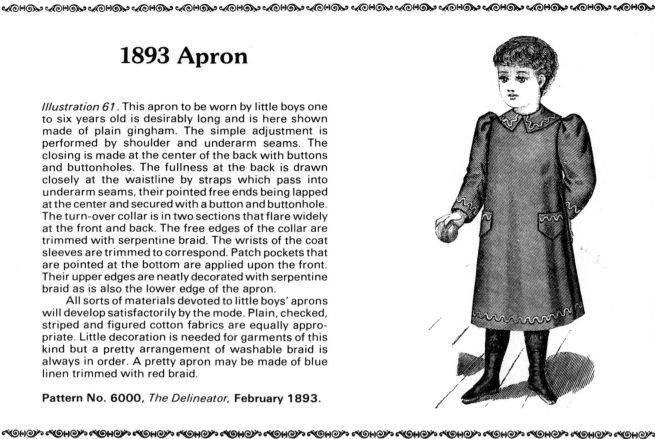

Illustration 61. This apron to be worn by little boys one to six years old is desirably long and is here shown made of plain gingham. The simple adjustment is performed by shoulder and underarm seams. The closing is made at the center of the back with buttons and buttonholes. The fullness at the back is drawn closely at the waistline by straps which pass into underarm seams, their pointed free ends being lapped at the center and secured with a button and buttonhole. The turn-over collar is in two sections that flare widely at the front and back. The free edges of the collar are trimmed with serpentine braid. The wrists of the coat sleeves are trimmed to correspond. Patch pockets that are pointed at the bottom are applied upon the front. Their upper edges are neatly decorated with serpentine braid as is also the lower edge of the apron.

All sorts of materials devoted to little boys' aprons will develop satisfactorily by the mode. Plain, checked, striped and figured cotton fabrics are equally appropriate. Little decoration is needed for garments of this kind but a pretty arrangement of washable braid is always in order. A pretty apron may be made of blue linen trimmed with red braid.

Pattern No. 6000, *The Delineator,* **February 1893.**

1893 Apron

Illustration 62. Checked gingham was chosen for this little boy's apron, sufficiently long to be wholly protective to the dress over which it is worn. It is worn by one to six year olds. The backs extend only a short distance below the waistline and are lengthened by a back skirt that falls with pretty fullness from gathers at the top. The fronts and backs are joined in shoulder and underarm seams. The closing is made at the center of the back with a button and buttonhole. The fanciful collar, which is in two sections that flare slightly at the front and back, is trimmed along its free edges with a row of white braid. Similar braid decorates the lower edge of the apron and upper edges of the patch pockets which are rounding at their lower corners. The full shirt-sleeves are gathered to wristbands which are ornamented with braid.

Striped, plain and checked gingham are generally used for aprons of this kind although chambray, percale and cross-barred muslin are also perfectly suited to the purpose. Soutache, cotton or serpentine braid or fancy stitching may be added for decoration, or a plain finish may be adopted.

Pattern No. 6001, *The Delineator,* **February 1893.**

Front View.   *Back View.*

1893 Child's Coat

Illustration 63. The child's coat for one to six year olds is illustrated here made of mahogany cloth and trimmed with black velvet ribbon. The skirt, which is hemmed at the front and lower edges, is gathered at the top and depends in soft, graceful folds from a short round body that is simply shaped by underarm and shoulder seams. The body is closed at the center of the front with buttons and buttonholes. The full puff sleeves are mounted upon coat-shaped linings which are revealed at the wrists with deep cuff effect, the exposed portions of the lining being faced with the material. The attractive cape consists of three graduated capes, the lowest of which extends well below the waistline. At the neck is a moderately high standing collar which is concealed by a full double box-plaited ruching of velvet, which, however, is only trimming. At the throat is a pretty bow of velvet ribbon, the long ends of which extend below the bottom of the cape.

These coats are very stylish and will develop attractively in cloth, serge, camel's hair, plaid, striped or checked suitings and in rough-surfaced goods of a seasonable texture. They may be attractively lined throughout with pretty plaid silk. The edges of the capes may be outlined with passementerie, gimp or bands of fur.

Pattern No. 4986, *The Delineator,* **February 1893.**

1893 Suit

Illustration 64. This suit is developed in a seasonable variety of cheviot. The fronts of the jacket join the seamless back in shoulder and underarm seams and are closed at the center. A plastron is buttoned to the fronts at both sides. About the waist is a belt that is in two sections, the pointed ends of which are lapped at the front and back. Buttonholes made in their front ends pass over one of the closing buttons of the plastron. The coat sleeves are of comfortable width; each is decorated at the back of the wrist with two

buttons. The collar is in rolling style with rounding ends. It is finished with machine-stitching. The free edges of the pocket laps which conceal the openings to side pockets are similarly completed. A single row of machine-stitching follows all the free edges of the jacket.

The trousers extend a little below the knees and are finished with hems. The customary seams and hip darts are introduced in their adjustment; the closing is made in a fly. Pockets are inserted in the outside leg seams. Two buttons decorate the lower end of each outside seam.

The jacket can be worn by three to ten-year-old boys. Five to sixteen-year-old boys will find this style of trousers appropriate.

The cap is made of cheviot. Its crown is composed of six triangular sections that meet in a point at the top. A peak or visor joins the cap both back and front; machine-stitching finishes the edges.

A smart suit may be developed by the mode in cloth, tricot, tweed, cheviot, mixed suiting and so forth. Machine-stitching or silk or mohair braid may finish the edges although a perfectly plain completion will be in best taste.

Pattern Nos. 6073 (Russian blouse jacket), 3783 (trousers) and 2175 (cap), *The Delineator,* **March 1893.**

1893 Suit

Illustration 65. The little boy's suit for two to six year olds is made of dark blue serge with machine-stitching for a finish. The jacket is shaped by center and side seams and is closed at the center of the front with buttons and buttonholes. Three side plaits arranged at each side of the closing are held in place by machine-stitching; the back is plaited to correspond. The coat sleeves are comfortably wide and are finished at the wrists with machine-stitching made to outline round cuffs. A rolling collar having rounding ends is at the neck. The right front is provided with a side pocket. A breast and a side pocket are inserted in the left front. The side pockets are finished with flaps and the breast pocket with a welt. All edges of the jacket are neatly finished with machine-stitching.

The trousers extend a trifle below the knees and are shaped by the usual seams and hip darts. The closing is made in a fly. Side pockets are inserted in the outside leg seams.

The jaunty polo cap has a circular crown to the edge of which the side is joined. It is lined with silk.

The suit may be developed in any fashionable variety of cloth, serge, cheviot, plaid or plain flannel, tweed and so forth. The cap may be of velvet, serge or corduroy and may match or contrast with the suit.

Pattern Nos. 6071 (jacket), 3783 (trousers) and 3167 (cap), *The Delineator,* **March 1893.**

1893 Sailor Suit

Illustration 66. In the present instance the sailor suit for boys two to eight years old is portrayed charmingly developed in white and blue flannel with white braid for decoration. The trousers extend a little below the knee and are shaped by the usual seams and hip darts. The legs are finished at the bottom with hems. Side pockets are inserted in the top of the outside leg seams. The closing is made in a fly. The top of the trousers is finished with a waistband which is attached to a sleeveless underwaist with buttons and button-holes. The underwaist is adjusted by shoulder seams. Its fronts are shaped to accommodate a shield which is buttoned on at each side.

The blouse, which is slipped on over the head, is shaped by shoulder and underarm seams. The lower edge is turned under for a hem in which a tape or elastic is inserted to draw the blouse to the waist, the fullness drooping in characteristic fashion. The front of the blouse is cut away in a deep V at the center to accommodate the long tapering ends of the deep sailor collar beneath which a polka dotted silk handkerchief is worn. The ends of the scarf are tied with a bow of white ribbon. The blue flannel shield disclosed between the ends of the collar is decorated with crosswise rows of white braid. The sleeves are very full and are each arranged at the top in a box plait. The fullness at the lower edge is collected in several box plaits that are stitched along their folds to round cuff depth. A handkerchief pocket is applied to the left front.

The cap is made of white flannel and suggests the Tam O'Shanter and sailor styles. The side shows a

seam at the center of the front and back and is sewn to the edge of the side and bears the word "Victor" in gold letters at the front. Its ends are joined in a seam at the back.

An attractive yachting suit may be developed by the mode in white flannel with trimmings of white or gold braid. Plain blue may be associated with blue and white striped variety for ordinary wear. White braid and embroidered nautical emblems and chevrons may provide garniture. The cap may match or contrast with the suit it accompanies.

Pattern Nos. 6005 (sailor suit) and 3033 (cap), *The Delineator,* **March 1893.**

1893 Suit

Illustration 67. Little boy's suit with vest buttoned in at the shoulders and under the arms.

Pattern No. 6003, *The Delineator,* **March 1893.**

Front View.

Back View.

Front View.

Front View.

Back View.

Back View.

1893 Dress

Illustration 68. Little boy's dress.

Pattern No. 6070, *The Delineator,* **March 1893.**

1893 Costume

Illustration 69. Boy's costume.

Pattern No. 6069, *The Delineator,* **March 1893.**

1893 Suit

Illustration 70. Blue and white serge are in this instance combined in the natty little dress for two to seven-year-old boys. White braid is used for garniture. The skirt, which extends to the knees and is deeply hemmed at the bottom, is laid in box plaits all round and depends from a long waisted body that is simply shaped by underarm and shoulder seams. The fronts flare broadly from the lower edge to the shoulders, disclosing a vest effectively between them. The vest is closed invisibly at the left side and is tastefully trimmed with curved rows of braid arranged in clusters of three. The sailor collar presents a square effect across the shoulders and has tapering ends that join the front edges of the fronts to the lower edge of the waist. Its free edges are neatly finished with a single row of machine-stitching. The joining of the body to the skirt is concealed by a shaped belt having a pointed overlapping end. It is passed through a slide and is finished along its outer edges with a single row of machine-stitching. The full sleeves are gathered at the top; the fullness at each wrist is laid at the back of the arm in forward and backward-turning plaits that extend to cuff depth and are stitched to position.

The cap is made of blue and white serge. The side shows a seam at the center of the front and back and is joined to the edge of the circular crown. The band is sewn to the lower edge of the side; its ends are joined in a seam at the back.

The dress will develop attractively in flannel of suitable weight, cloth, tricot and other fabrics devoted to little boys' wear. Worsted braid will usually be employed for decoration. Embroidered anchors, stars and other nautical emblems may ornament the collar and the upper portion of the vest. The cap may match the suit or contrast prettily with it.

Pattern Nos. 6138 (dress) and 3033 (cap), *The Delineator,* **May 1893.**

1893 Dress

Illustration 71. The dress is an attractive style for small boys and is here developed in dark blue flannel. It is also shown in *Illustration 70.*

Pattern No. 6138, *The Delineator,* **May 1893.**

Front View.

Back View.

1893 Blouse Suit

Illustration 72. Blouse suits are always admired for little boys. The suit fashioned for two to eight year olds is here pictured made of white India silk and black velvet and is especially attractive. The blouse is cut from India silk and has a seamless yoke that is square at the back and rounding in front and is cut away at the front to accommodate a short shield. The shield is prettily trimmed with cross rows of braid. The full back and fronts depend from the yoke and are joined in underarm seams; the fullness is arranged at the top in backward-turning plaits at each side of the center of the back and in forward-turning plaits at each side of the closing which is made at the center of the front with buttonholes and buttons. The blouse droops in regulation fashion and is turned under and stitched at the bottom to form a casing through which tapes are passed to hold the garment well into the figure. At the neck is a turnover collar, the tapering ends of which meet below the shield. A bow of ribbon is placed over the closing just below the shield. The free edge of the collar is prettily trimmed with a frill of embroidered edging. The full sleeves are finished with narrow wristbands which are concealed by rolling cuffs that are prettily rounded at the outside of the arm. The free edges of the cuffs are trimmed with frills of embroidered edging.

The trousers are made of black velvet. They are made without a fly and are shaped by the usual seams along the inside and outside of the legs and by a seam at the center of the front and back. They extend to the knees and are closed at the sides.

The cap is also made of velvet and has a hexagonal crown joined to a band which fits the head closely. A tassel is attached to the center of the crown and droops jauntily at the right side.

The blouse may be made of India or China silk, surah, linen lawn, figured batiste, white French percale or fine nainsook. It may be trimmed with lace, fine embroidery or rows of feather-stitching. Velvet, corduroy, cheviot, diagonal, tweed, fancy mixed suiting, and so forth may be used for the trousers. The cap may be made of the same kind of material as the trousers or may contrast effectively with them, as preferred.

Pattern Nos. 6139 (blouse), 4197 (trousers) and 6075 (cap), *The Delineator,* **May 1893.**

Front View.

Back View.

1893 Blouse

Illustration 73. The blouse, which may accompany skirts or knee trousers, is here shown made of fine white cambric and trimmed with frills of white embroidered edging. A variation of this blouse appears in *Illustration 72.*

Pattern No. 6139, *The Delineator,* **May 1893.**

1893 Sailor Suit

Illustration 74. This costume consists of a sailor blouse and sailor trousers and is shown made of navy blue and white serge. The blouse is made on a supporting underwaist, the use of which, however, is optional. The blouse and underwaist are shaped by shoulder and underarm seams. Their lower edges are gathered and joined to a belt upon which buttons are sewn for the attachment of the trousers. When the underwaist is omitted, the lower edge of the blouse is turned under and stitched to form a casing through which an elastic is run to regulate the fullness, the blouse drooping in the usual manner. The fronts are reversed at the top by the collar; the neck is filled in by a shield of white serge which is attached with buttons and buttonholes at each side and may be omitted if an open neck be preferred. The collar is in the regulation sailor shape, falling deep and square at the back and is finished with a single row of machine-stitching which is continued along the front edge of the overlapping front. The closing is made invisibly at the center of the front. A patch pocket applied to the left front is decorated with machine-stitching and a single row of stitching outlines a round cuff upon the shapely coat sleeve. The sleeve is further ornamented with two buttons placed at the back of the arm. The shield is trimmed at the top with four rows of blue braid arranged to follow its curving upper edge. The blouse is appropriate for seven to sixteen-year-old boys.

The trousers, to be worn by boys three to sixteen years of age, are in true sailor style, displaying the usual flare over the boot. They are shaped by the customary leg seams and by a seam at the center of the front and back. The fronts are made with a fall-bearer, the closing being made in regulation style at the sides and across the front with buttonholes and buttons. A pocket is inserted in the right back; a strap and buckle adjust the trousers comfortably to the size of the waist.

The suit will develop attractively in white or blue flannel or serge or in a combination of the two colors. For little boys piqué, duck, percale and galatea are much admired. The finish may be provided by braid or machine-stitching and anchors, stars, wheels and so forth may decorate the blouse.

The hat is a straw sailor banded with blue ribbon.

Pattern No. 6360, *The Delineator,* **August 1893.**

1893 Dress

Illustration 75. The little dress for boys two to seven years old is developed in tan duck and is a sensible garment for small boys as its simplicity of construction renders it very easy to launder. It reaches to a becoming depth and is closed diagonally all the way down, the fronts being shaped to lap widely at the top. The back is gracefully curved to the form by a center seam that terminates at the waistline above extra fullness underfolded in a broad box plait. The shapely coat sleeves show double rows of machine-stitching made at deep cuff depth. The rolling collar is finished with a single row of similar stitching. The patch pockets are each completed with a double row of stitching at the upper edge and a single row at the other edges. Straps are included in the underarm seams at the waistline; their pointed ends are lapped at the center of the back and fastened with a buttonhole and button. The straps are finished with stitchings.

The cap, which suggests the Tam O'Shanter shape, is made of cloth and has a circular crown to which the sides are joined. The band is sewn to the loose edge of the sides and a silk lining is added. The cap is decorated at the top with a silk pompon.

The little dress is an extremely comfortable style for warm weather and will make up attractively in piqué, Marseilles, linen duck, percale, gingham and many other fabrics of a washable nature. All sorts of woolens are also well adapted to the mode and, if a more fanciful completion be desired, any pretty arrangement of fancy braid may be applied. The cap may match or contrast with the dress and may be developed in any preferred variety of woolen goods.

Pattern No. 6361 (dress) and 3033 (cap), *The Delineator,* **August 1893.**

1893 Sailor Suit

Illustration 76. Navy blue and white duck were selected for the suit for two to twelve-year-old boys. Machine-stitching, soutache braid, buttons and a ribbon bow comprise the decorations. The blouse may be made up with or without a supporting underwaist. Its fronts are reversed at the neck by a deep sailor collar and to the fronts, underneath, is buttoned a shield which, however, may be omitted if an open neck is preferred. When the underwaist is used, the lower edge of the blouse and underwaist are gathered and joined to a belt to which buttons are sewn to attach the trousers. When the underwaist is not desired, the lower edge of the blouse is turned under to form a casing through which an elastic is inserted to regulate the fullness. The shield is trimmed at the top with two curved rows of blue braid below which is set a dark blue star ornament. The full sleeves are gathered at the top and bottom and finished with pointed cuffs which are closed at the back of the arm with buttons. Ribbon ties are tacked beneath the ends of the collar and arranged in a natty bow at the closing which is made with buttonholes and buttons. The edges of the collar and cuffs are finished with machine-stitching. Stitching finishes a welt that conceals a pocket opening at the left side.

The trousers follow closely the outline of the figure. They are made without a fly and are shaped by the usual seams along the inside and outside of the legs and by a seam at the center of the front and back. They extend to the knee and are closed at the sides. Buttons are applied at the lower part of the outside seams.

The cap has a hexagonal crown, the edge of which is joined to a band. A tassel is attached to the center of the crown and droops prettily at the left side.

The suit may be developed in serge, flannel, lightweight cloth, cheviot, tweed, galatea or piqué, the favorite hues being blue and white, either in solid colors or in stripes. Nautical emblems such as anchors, wheels and so forth may be embroidered on the collar and vest with rope silk.

Pattern No. 6359 (blouse), 4197 (trousers) and 6075 (cap), *The Delineator*, **August 1893.**

1893 Sailor Suit

Illustration 77. Dark blue serge is the material in this suit for boys three to twelve years old. The trousers, which reach a trifle below the knee, are shaped by the customary seams along the inside and outside of the leg and at the center of the front and back. Darts at the back secure a perfect adjustment at the top and pockets are made at the sides and in the right side of the back. The upper part of the trousers is finished with a waistband. Buttonholes are worked in the waistband to pass over corresponding buttons which are sewn to the underwaist and the closing is made at the sides.

The blouse is made up on a supporting underwaist which may be omitted if deemed undesirable. The blouse and underwaist are shaped by underarm and shoulder seams. Their lower edges are gathered and joined to a belt upon which buttons are sewn for the attachment of the trousers. When the underwaist is omitted, the lower edge of the blouse is turned under for a hem through which an elastic is run to regulate the fullness, the blouse drooping in the usual manner. The fronts are rolled back at the top by a collar between which is revealed a shield that is attached with buttons and buttonholes at each side. The collar is in true sailor shape, falling deep and square at the back. It is covered with a facing that is extended down the front edges of the fronts to form underfacings. The closing is made invisibly at the center of the front and a row of white braid simulates a pointed cuff upon each of the shapely coat sleeves. The left sleeve is further ornamented with a chevron and anchor. The shield is decorated with four curved rows of braid and a row of similar braid outlines the sailor collar and covers each outside seam of the trousers. A bow of ribbon is placed below the ends of the sailor collar.

Blue or white flannel or serge or a combination of the two colors will make up attractively in the suit. For small boys piqué, duck, percale and galatea will be greatly favored. The finish may be provided by machine-stitching and anchors, stars, wheels and so forth may decorate the blouse. A stylish suit of this description may be made of all-white flannel and neatly finished with machine-stitching.

The hat is a straw sailor showing a blue ribbon band and streamers.

Pattern No. 6441, *The Delineator,* **September 1893.**

Front View.   *Back View.*

1893 Sailor Suit

Illustration 78. This is the same sailor suit depicted in *Illustration 77.* In this instance the costume is made of blue and white serge.

Pattern No. 6441, *The Delineator,* **September 1893.**

1893 Suit

Illustration 79. Red and white flannel and fancy cashmere are attractively associated in this smart little costume. Boys two to six years of age will wear this fashionably. The kilt skirt is hemmed at the bottom; its deep plaits all turn in the same direction and are well pressed in their folds. The top of the skirt is lapped upon the high necked sleeveless underwaist to which it may be stitched or attached with buttons and buttonholes. The underwaist is shaped by underarm and shoulder seams and closed at the center of the back. The neck is finished with a close fitting standing collar.

    The blouse is shaped with underarm and shoulder seams. The fronts are in V outline at the top to receive the tapering ends of the sailor collar which presents the characteristic square outline at the back. The ends of the collar meet under a bow of ribbon below which the closing is made invisibly. The bottom of the waist is finished with a hem through which an elastic or tape is passed to draw the fullness well into the waist and cause it to droop below in regulation fashion. The sleeves are of comfortable width. Each wrist is finished with a round cuff.

    The cap is made of red and white flannel and has a circular crown that is interlined with one or two thicknesses of crinoline or canvas. To the crown are joined the sides which are seamed together at the center of the front and back. The band is sewn to the loose edges of the sides and meets at the back beneath a bow of ribbon. The front of the band is decorated with lettering embroidered with silk. The entire cap is lined with silk.

    The suit may be developed in serge, flannel, galatea, piqué, gingham or percale and combinations will make up with particularly good effect. Machine-stitching may follow the edges. Nautical emblems may ornament the corners of the collar and the front of the underwaist revealed with the effect of a shield. The cap may match the costume or be made of a widely contrasting material.

Pattern Nos. 6440 (costume) and 3003 (cap), *The Delineator,* **September 1893.**

Front View.   Back View.

1893 Suit

Illustration 80. Fancy cashmere and plain white and red flannel are combined in this costume. It is developed differently in *Illustration 79.*

Pattern No. 6440, *The Delineator,* **September 1893.**

Front View.   Back View.

1893 Overcoat

Illustration 81. Boy's overcoat.

Pattern No. 6444, *The Delineator,* **September 1893.**

1893 Ulster

Illustration 82. This little boy's ulster is made of fancy cheviot and plain velvet; it is fashionable for boys two to seven years of age. Its fronts are closed to the throat in double-breasted style with buttons and buttonholes and are rendered smooth at the sides by long underarm darts. The back is nicely conformed to the figure by a curving center seam that terminates at the waistline above long coat laps and by side seams that disappear at the top of the long coat plaits. The sleeves are comfortably wide and are plainly finished at the wrists. At the neck is a velvet rolling collar beneath which is attached a cape that is fitted smoothly on the shoulders by darts. The free edges of the cape are finished with machine-stitching and so are the front and lower edges of the coat. Pocket laps cover the openings to side pockets inserted in the fronts. A breast pocket in the left front is finished with a welt. The loose edges of the pocket laps are followed with a single row of machine-stitching.

The ulster extends below the kilt or knee trousers with which it is worn and will, therefore, be a popular garment for use in stormy weather. It will make up satisfactorily in melton, cloth, cheviot, homespun, frieze, kersey and rough-surfaced coatings of all kinds.

The felt hat has a ribbon band and a bow at the left side.

Pattern No. 6443, *The Delineator,* **September 1893.**

1893 Overcoat

Illustration 83. The little boy's overcoat to be worn by two to seven year olds is developed in light melton. It is fashioned in a jaunty style that is particularly becoming to small boys and is well adapted to accompany kilt skirts. It extends to below the knee and its fronts lap closely and are closed to the thoat in double-breasted fashion with buttons and buttonholes. The back extends to the waistline and is lengthened by a skirt portion which is arranged in two box plaits between two side plaits. The seam joining the back and skirt portion is concealed by a strap having pointed ends. The sleeves are comfortably wide. A cuff is outlined on each with a fanciful arrangement of soutache braid. At the neck is a rolling collar with widely flaring ends. The edges of the collar are followed with soutache braid which is coiled at the corners. The triple cape is fitted smoothly on the shoulders by darts and is attached beneath the rolling collar. It flares widely at the front. The free edges are trimmed with soutache braid which is coiled at each lower front corner. Pocket laps cover openings to side pockets inserted in the fronts. The curved opening to a breast pocket in each front is finished with machine-stitching.

The Scotch cap matches the coat. Its oval crown is joined to the side which is narrowest at the back where the ends meet in a seam. The cap is creased through the center in regulation style, is interlined with canvas and lined with satin. It is decorated at the edge with a band of ribbon, the ends of which fall loosely at the back.

All sorts of plain and fancy overcoatings are appropriate for top garments of this kind. Such a coat is especially adaptable to the intermediate seasons for which it may be developed in light textured cloth, cheviot, diagonal or kersey. The cap may contrast with the coat and will usually be ribbon-trimmed.

Pattern Nos. 6435 (overcoat) and 3636 (cap), *The Delineator*, **September 1893.**

1893 Suit

Illustration 84. The pea jacket, which is here portrayed made of chinchilla, is a comfortable top garment for school or best wear, for little boys from three to eight years old. Its fronts are reversed at the top in small lapels that meet the rolling collar in notches. It is closed in double-breasted style with buttons and buttonholes. The fronts join the seamless back in side seams that are discontinued a short distance above the lower edge at the top of extra widths allowed on the fronts for underlaps. Cuffs are outlined on the shapely sleeves with braid. Similar braid decorates the lapels and the front and lower edges of the jacket. A buttonhole is made in each lapel. The rolling collar is covered with a facing of velvet. Pocket laps cover the openings to side pockets inserted in the fronts and a change pocket in the right front. They are ornamented at their free edges with braid. Braid also finishes a welt at the opening of a breast pocket in the left side.

The trousers are made of cheviot, extend to just below the knee and are shaped by the usual seams. They are closed at the sides with buttons and buttonholes and are fitted smoothly at the top by the customary darts. Pockets are inserted above the side seams. Buttonholes are made in the waistband, finishing the top to be passed over buttons on the underwaist or blouse.

The jaunty polo cap is made of cloth and has a circular crown to the edge of which are joined the sides. The cap is lined with silk.

The pea jacket may be developed in any variety of coating such as mixed, striped or checked cheviot, melton, kersey or smooth or rough-surfaced cloth. A finish of machine-stitching is usually preferred. The trousers may be developed in any kind of plain or fancy suiting, cloth, cheviot, corduroy or serge. The cap may match or contrast with the coat.

Pattern Nos. 6438 (pea jacket), 3163 (trousers) and 3167 (cap), *The Delineator*, **September 1893.**

1893 Costumes

Illustration 85. Two costumes for boys which appeared in a Butterick advertisement in *The Delineator,* circa 1893.

Left: Pattern Nos. 3230 (costume) and 3167 (cap).
Right: Pattern Nos. 3230 (costume), 3229 (jacket) and 3033 (cap). *The Delineator,* circa 1893.

1894 Suit

Illustration 86. This costume is made of striped and plain galatea, plain white cambric and all-over embroidery. It can be worn by little men from two to seven years of age. The skirt is arranged in uniform kilt plaits all round and is attached with buttonholes and buttons to a sleeveless underwaist that is shaped by shoulder seams and closed at the center of the front with buttonholes and buttons.

The blouse, which is made of cambric, is shaped by shoulder and underarm seams and closed at the center of the front with buttonholes and buttons that are concealed by a double jabot of embroidered edging arranged upon the overlapping front. The lower edge of the blouse is turned under to form a hem in which a tape or elastic is inserted to draw the fullness to the figure and cause the garment to droop in regulation fashion below the short jacket. The shirt-sleeves are gathered to wrist bands over which are reversed round cuffs that are trimmed with frills of embroidered edging. At the neck is a sailor collar of all-over embroidery decorated at the edge with a frill of edging.

The fronts of the jacket are rolled back in lapels which pass into the shoulder seams and are covered with facings of plain white galatea. The back is fitted by a center seam and is separated from the fronts by side-back gores. The side-back seams are left open for a short distance at their lower ends. The sleeves are in coat-sleeve shape; the cuffs of the blouse are rolled back over them. The sailor collar is worn outside the jacket. Each lapel is decorated with a row of buttons applied along its outer edge.

The Tam O'Shanter hat is made of striped galatea with the headband of the plain fabric.

Plain, mottled, checked or fancy suiting of any kind, duck, piqué and so forth will make up attractively in a suit of this style with lace, nainsook or cambric for the blouse. The jacket may be trimmed with braid or a plain completion may be chosen.

Pattern Nos. 6921 (costume) and 3033 (cap), *The Delineator,* **June 1894.**

Front View.　　　　　　Back View.

1894 Costume

Illustration 87. Plain and plaid cloth and white lawn are here associated in the jaunty costume which may be used for best or everyday wear according to the material employed in its construction. The blouse in this instance is made of lawn. This costume is developed differently in *Illustration 86*.

Pattern No. 6921, *The Delineator*, **June 1894**.

Front View.

Back View.

1894 Suit

Illustration 89. The suit is here developed in dark blue cloth and fine white lawn. It is shown differently in *Illustration 88*.

Pattern No. 6922, *The Delineator*, **June 1894**.

1894 Suit

Illustration 88. Lightweight suiting and white surah are united in the jaunty suit with lace frills, braid and buttons for garniture. Designed for two to seven-year-old boys, the trousers reach to the knee and are shaped by hip darts and the usual seams along the outside and inside of the leg. They are closed at the sides, have pockets inserted above the outside leg seams and are attached with buttonholes and buttons to a sleeveless underwaist that is comfortably adjusted by shoulder seams and closed at the center of the front. Three buttons decorate each leg in front of the outside seam.

The blouse, which is made of surah, is shaped by the customary shoulder and underarm seams and closed at the center of the front beneath a double jabot of lace edging. The lower edge of the blouse is turned under for a hem; a tape or elastic inserted in the hem draws the fullness about the waist, the blouse drooping softly below the short jacket. The shirt-sleeves are finished with wristbands and round cuffs that are trimmed with lace frills. At the neck is a narrow band from which a deep sailor collar with widely flaring ends falls prettily. The collar is decorated with a frill of lace to match the cuffs.

The Eton jacket is fashionably short and is gracefully shaped by underarm gores and a curving center seam. The fronts are reversed by a rolling collar; the collar and the reversed portions of the fronts are covered with a facing of cloth which is continued for underfacings to the lower edge of the jacket. The coat sleeves are sufficiently wide to slip on easily over those of the blouse, the cuffs of which are rolled back over the jacket sleeves. The collar of the blouse is worn outside the jacket. The front and lower edges of the jacket are trimmed with two rows of braid crossed in basket fashion at the corners.

The suit is very natty and will be developed in handsome material for dressy wear. The trousers and jacket will make up nicely in cloth, serge or plain or fancy suiting of seasonable weight. China or India silk or lawn may be chosen for the blouse.

The hat is a Tam O'Shanter of fine straw.

Pattern No. 6922, *The Delineator*, **June 1894**.

1894 Costumes

Illustration 90. This blouse and jacket are portrayed in two different costumes. A picturesque suit for a small boy two to seven years old may consist of a blouse and jacket of this kind and either knee trousers or a kilt, as the years of the little man demand. The blouse, which is shown in the present instance developed in fine lawn, is fashioned in the simple manner usually observed in garments of this class. The shaping is accomplished by shoulder and underarm seams; the closing is made at the center of the front. The hem of the overlapping front is decorated with a fluted frill of the material that is gathered through the center under a feather-stitched band. The lower edge of the blouse is hemmed to form a casing through which a tape is run to draw the garment closely to the figure, the fullness drooping in the usual manner. The full shirt-sleeves are gathered at the top and bottom and finished with wristbands and round cuffs that are joined to the wristbands and completed with frills, the cuffs being turned back over the sleeves of the jacket. At the neck is a deep rolling collar mounted upon a shaped band and finished at the edge with a frill of the lawn.

The removable jacket is made of dark green cloth. The back is shaped by a center seam and is joined to the front in underarm and shoulder seams. The three seams at the back are terminated a short distance above the lower edge; the corners are prettily rounded. The fronts are closed at the throat with a hook and eye and flare gradually below, being rounded gracefully toward the back. The sleeves, which are shaped by inside and outside seams, are comfortably wide. The fullness at the lower edge is collected in side plaits that flare prettily upward beneath the pointed rolling cuffs which are ornamented at the outside of the arm with tiny pearl buttons. All the free edges of the jacket are bound with black mohair braid; the fronts are decorated with tiny pearl buttons sewn just back of their edges. A pocket is inserted in the left front and its edges are bound with braid.

The blouse may be developed in cambric, chambray, lawn or nainsook and for the jacket any pretty variety of plain cloth, serge, hopsacking or vienna may be chosen. The jacket and the kilt it accompanies may be of red, dark blue, green or black goods and may be finished with machine-stitching or braid.

The kilt is here shown developed in dark blue serge. It may accompany a blouse or shirtwaist and jacket to complete a natty house, street or school suit for a small boy. It reaches to the usual depth and may be arranged with a broad box plait at the front and kilt plaits at the sides and back, or may be disposed in kilt plaits all round. The top of the kilt is finished with an under-waistband in which buttonholes are made to pass over corresponding buttons sewn to the under-waist. The closing is made underneath a plait at the right side of the front. When the kilt is made with a box plait at the front, a row of buttons is decoratively applied along each fold of the box plait.

A kilt of this kind may be developed in cloth, flannel, sacking, cheviot and various other woolens of seasonable texture. It may be worn with a shirt-blouse of silk or cambric and an Eton jacket of cloth. It will usually be finished as represented in the present instance.

Pattern Nos. 7202 (jacket), 4197 (knee trousers), 3033 (cap), 7201 (kilt) and 7199 (octagonal hat), *The Delineator,* **November 1894.**

Front View.

Back View.

Front View.

Back View.

Back View.

Front View.

The cap is of gray cloth and consists of two sections, a band that fits the head closely and a crown which joins the band and is shaped by a seam at the center of the front and back and a seam at both sides to present the regulation mortarboard shape. A silk tassel droops over the cap at the left side with a pretty effect.

All kinds of suitings in plain, mottled and mixed effects may be chosen for a suit of this kind. However, preference will often be given to plain cloth in dark blue, green or gray. Military ornaments formed of black braid may decorate the jacket or a simple completion may, if preferred, be chosen.

Pattern Nos. 7445 (jacket), 3163 (knee trousers) and 4393 (cap), *The Delineator,* **March 1895.**

1895 Suit

Illustration 91. This suit introduces a jacket fashioned in military style, the effect of which is intensified by the choice of military gray cloth with black braid for decoration. The jacket for three to eight years olds is becomingly long and is simply shaped by shoulder and side seams, the side seams being curved to define the form becomingly. The fronts are closed at the throat and separate gradually all the way down. They are trimmed along their front edges with military braid arranged in a single row and at intervals in frog designs. The braid is continued along the lower edge of the jacket and also appears in three frog designs upon the coat sleeves above the wrist. The openings to side pockets inserted in the fronts are covered with fancifully shaped pocket laps that are trimmed at their free edges with braid. The rolling collar, which forms a becoming neck completion, is covered by the deep rolling collar of the shirtwaist.

The short trousers reach to the knee and are shaped by hip darts and the customary seams along the outside and inside of the leg. They can be worn by boys from ages three to ten. The closing is made at the sides. The trousers are provided with the usual number of pockets and are finished at the top with a waistband and attached to the shirtwaist with buttonholes and buttons.

1895 Outdoor Suit

Illustration 92. Little boy's outdoor suit consisting of a jacket, kilt and cap.

Pattern Nos. 7441 (jacket), 7201 (kilt) and 6075 (cap), *The Delineator,* **March 1895.**

1895 Norfolk Costume

Illustration 93. Little boy's Norfolk costume.

Pattern No. 7446, *The Delineator,* **March 1895.**

Front View.   *Back View.*

1895 Norfolk Costume

Illustration 94. Little boy's Norfolk costume. A different development is shown in *Illustration 93.*

Pattern No. 7446, *The Delineator,* **March 1895.**

1895 Suit

Illustration 95. Blue serge and white flannel were effectively associated in the present development of this suit, machine-stitching providing a neat finish. The jacket to be worn by boys two to nine years old is also known as the "skipper" jacket and introduces some of the features of the popular reefer modes. The fronts close in double-breasted fashion with button-holes and buttons and are joined to the back in shoulder and underarm seams while the back is nicely curved to the figure by a center seam. The fronts are reversed at the top by the white sailor collar which falls in regulation square outline at the back and curves prettily over the shoulders. The collar is finished with a single row of machine-stitching. The front and lower edges of the jacket and the edges of the pocket laps which cover openings to side pockets inserted in the fronts are similarly finished. A row of stitching is made above each coat sleeve to outline a round cuff.

The knee trousers are close fitting and button at the sides. They are decorated at the lower part of each outside seam with three buttons. The trouser pattern will fit boys from two to ten years old.

The jaunty polo cap has a circular crown to the edge of which is joined the side. It is made of blue cloth and lined with silk.

The suit may be developed in any fashionable variety of cloth, serge, plain or twilled flannel, corduroy, velvet and so forth. Machine-stitching or silk or worsted braid may contribute a neat finish. The cap may be of the same material as the jacket and trousers or may contrast effectively.

Pattern Nos. 7447 (sailor jacket), 4197 (knee trousers) and 3167 (cap), *The Delineator,* **March 1895.**

1895 Suit

Illustration 96. A very natty spring or summer suit for a boy is here developed in lightweight cheviot, the jacket being neatly finished with machine-stitching. The jacket for three to eight-year-old boys displays an applied box plait at each side of the center of the front and back the box plaits at the back are arranged over the curved side seams which, with underarm and shoulder seams, render the jacket very shapely. The fronts are reversed at the top in lapels that meet the rolling collar in notches while the closing is made in single-breasted style below the lapels with buttonholes and bone buttons. The jacket is provided with a belt which has rounding ends closed at the center of the front with a buttonhole and button. Patch pockets are stitched to the fronts near the bottom, back of the box plaits. The coat sleeves are comfortably wide; each is finished with two rows of machine-stitching made to outline a round cuff while a single row of stitching finishes the front and lower edges of the jacket.

The trousers, appropriate for boys three to ten years of age, are in full knickerbocker or bloomer style and are shaped by the customary seams and hip darts and closed with a fly. They extend just below the knees and the legs are finished with underfacings that form casings for elastic straps which draw the lower edges closely below the knee, the fullness drooping in the usual bloomer style. The trousers have lap-covered pockets at the back and inserted pockets in the side seams and are finished at the top with a waistband stitched underneath. Straps are arranged on the outside to support a belt.

The cap matches the jacket and trousers. It has a circular crown to which the sides are joined. The band is joined to the loose edge of the sides. The cap has a silk lining.

Pattern Nos. 7444 (jacket), 7136 (trousers) and 3033 (cap), *The Delineator,* **March 1895.**

1895 Middy Suit

Illustration 97. The middy suit occupies a leading place among the modes for small boys from three to ten years old. In its present development of dark blue and white serge with a decoration of white braid and brass buttons, it is especially attractive as well as serviceable. The trousers are of comfortable width in the leg and present the nautical flare over the boot. They are closed at the sides and are provided with the usual side pockets.

The sleeveless vest of white serge is shaped by shoulder and underarm seams and closed at the back with buttonholes and buttons. It is completed with a neckband and decorated with an emblem wrought in blue Asiatic silk.

The fronts of the jaunty jacket separate with a gradual flare and extend to a little below the vest. The back, which shapes a short point at the center, is closely fitted by side-back gores and a center seam. The sailor collar has long tapering ends and its free edges are decorated with a row of wide white braid between two rows of narrow braid. The sleeves are comfortably wide and are finished a little above the wrist with a row of wide braid between two encircling rows of narrow braid, two small brass buttons in front of the outside seam completing the decoration. Four large brass buttons adorn each jacket front below the collar and machine-stitching finishes the lower and front edges of the jacket.

Serge, cloth, cheviot, piqué and duck are all adaptable to the mode; the finish may be machine-stitching with decorations of braid. The vest should, to be effective, have an embroidered emblem wrought heavily with embroidery silk.

The middy cap is of duck with blue ribbon about its band.

Pattern No. 7702, *The Delineator,* **June 1895.**

1895 Costume

Illustration 98. White piqué and blue duck is the combination seen in this handsome little costume for two to seven year olds. The skirt reaches to a becoming depth and is finished at the bottom with a hem and arranged in kilt plaits all round. It is attached with buttons and buttonholes to a sleeveless underwaist that is fitted by shoulder seams and closed in front with buttonholes and buttons.

The blouse is shaped by shoulder and underarm seams and closed invisibly at the center of the front. The lower edge is turned under for a hem in which a tape is inserted to draw it closely about the waist, the blouse drooping in the usual fashion. The fronts are reversed quite low by the deep sailor collar which tapers to points; at the ends of the collar a ribbon is arranged in a sailor knot. In the open neck is seen a shield of blue duck which is buttoned in and decorated with an embroidered emblem formed of a star above chevrons, a row of stitching finishing the neck edge. The novel sleeves display a broad box plait on the upper side extending from the top of the straight round cuffs which are closed with buttonholes and buttons below the short openings at the outside seam. The edges of the collar and cuffs are finished with a row of machine-stitching. A patch pocket with round lower corners is applied on the left front.

Stylish and serviceable little suits for summer may be made up by the mode in linen duck or cotton duck, piqué, galatea, cheviot, percale or grass linen. Braid or machine-stitching may be used as a decoration.

The straw hat is in Tam O'Shanter style with a ribbon about its band.

Pattern No. 7703, *The Delineator,* **June 1895.**

1895 Child's Bathing Costumes

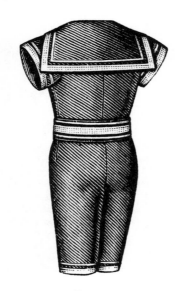

Front View.

Back View.

Illustrations 99 and 100. Two styles of child's bathing costumes are illustrated, one being close-fitting; the other is characterized by a very pretty fullness. Navy blue flannel was selected for both costumes with a decoration of white braid. The close-fitting costume is shaped by shoulder seams, underarm darts, inside leg seams in the drawers which are extensions of the body and a center seam. The closing is made to a desirable depth at the center of the front with buttons and buttonholes. The very short cap sleeves have seams under the arms and are edged with a row of narrow braid above a row of wide braid. Similar decoration is applied to the lower edges of the drawers. The fronts are cut slightly low at the top to accommodate the ends of the sailor collar which falls in regulation square outline across the back. It is decorated to correspond with the sleeves. A wide belt encircling the waist has a pointed overlapping end and is made decorative by a band of wide braid at the center and narrow braid at the edges.

The body of the full costume is also extended to form the drawers and the shaping is accomplished by shoulder seams, inside leg seams and a center seam. The closing is made at the center of the front with buttons and buttonholes. The fullness in the body is drawn into the figure at the waistline by a tape inserted in a casing. The drawers are finished in knickerbocker style, being drawn in by tapes inserted in casings made far enough from the lower edges to form frills. The short puff sleeves are gathered at the top and drawn in by tapes inserted in casings made a little above the lower edge to form frills. A row of wide and a row of narrow braid decorate the lower edge of each sleeve. The neck is finished with a broad sailor collar that falls in square outline at the back and joins the front edges of the fronts which are shaped in a very slight V. The collar is decorated at the edge with a row of wide and a row of narrow braid and the lower edges of the drawers are trimmed to correspond. A wide belt encircles the waist and is closed at the front. It has pointed ends and its edges are followed by a row of narrow braid, a row of wide braid being applied at the center.

Flannel in dark blue or gray shades is usually selected for bathing costumes. Red or white braid is a favored trimming. When a bright effect is desired, dark red cloth may be used for the collar and sleeves. A dainty child-like costume may be of white serge with a decoration of narrow blue or red washable braid.

Pattern No. 7700, *The Delineator,* **June 1895.**

Front View.

Back View.

1895 Sailor Costume

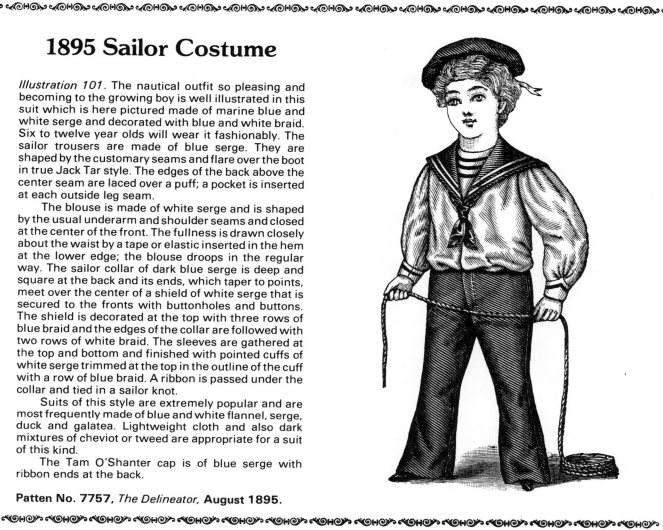

Illustration 101. The nautical outfit so pleasing and becoming to the growing boy is well illustrated in this suit which is here pictured made of marine blue and white serge and decorated with blue and white braid. Six to twelve year olds will wear it fashionably. The sailor trousers are made of blue serge. They are shaped by the customary seams and flare over the boot in true Jack Tar style. The edges of the back above the center seam are laced over a puff; a pocket is inserted at each outside leg seam.

The blouse is made of white serge and is shaped by the usual underarm and shoulder seams and closed at the center of the front. The fullness is drawn closely about the waist by a tape or elastic inserted in the hem at the lower edge; the blouse droops in the regular way. The sailor collar of dark blue serge is deep and square at the back and its ends, which taper to points, meet over the center of a shield of white serge that is secured to the fronts with buttonholes and buttons. The shield is decorated at the top with three rows of blue braid and the edges of the collar are followed with two rows of white braid. The sleeves are gathered at the top and bottom and finished with pointed cuffs of white serge trimmed at the top in the outline of the cuff with a row of blue braid. A ribbon is passed under the collar and tied in a sailor knot.

Suits of this style are extremely popular and are most frequently made of blue and white flannel, serge, duck and galatea. Lightweight cloth and also dark mixtures of cheviot or tweed are appropriate for a suit of this kind.

The Tam O'Shanter cap is of blue serge with ribbon ends at the back.

Patten No. 7757, *The Delineator,* **August 1895.**

1895 Child's Coat

Front View.   *Back View.*

Illustration 102. A novel feature of this child's long coat is the monk's hood which forms a deep round collar in front and adds to the picturesque effect. Forest green cloth was here selected for the coat with plaid silk for the hood lining. The coat has a short-waisted body shaped by underarm and shoulder seams and closed at the center of the front with buttons and buttonholes. The straight full skirt, which is deeply hemmed at the bottom and narrowly at the front edges, is gathered at the top and joined to the waist, falling in soft folds about the figure. A rolling collar completes the neck, its square ends flaring effectively. The monk's hood, which may be used or not as desired, is shaped by a seam that extends from the center to the outer edge. It is prettily reversed by a backward-turning plait at each side of the center at the top. Between the plaits the top is gathered. The collar, which the hood forms in front, lies smoothly and is faced with the cloth, the plaid lining being only in the hood portion.

Pattern No. 7825, *The Delineator,* **September 1895.**

Front View.   Back View.

1895 Child's Coat

Illustration 103. This child's coat, which may be made up with or without the ripple cape collars, is illustrated made of red cloth and decorated with machine-stitching. The waist is shaped by shoulder and under-arm seams and is closed at the center of the front underneath, a broad box plait formed on the front edge of the right front. A row of buttons decorates each fold of the plait. The stylish circular skirt has bias back edges joined in a center seam. A broad box plait is laid at each side of the seam and the overlapping front edge. It is joined smoothly to the waist and falls in ripples at the sides. Two circular cape collars are included in the seam with a rolling collar that has flaring ends. Both cape collars fall in stylish ripples all round and terminate underneath the box plait. Large square-cornered pocket laps located on the sides of the skirt produce a very attractive effect. The large leg-o'-mutton sleeves are shaped by inside and outside seams and are fashionably full at the top and close fitting on the forearm. A belt of the material with pointed ends encircles the waist and closes at the center of the front. A row of machine-stitching finishes all the edges of the coat. The small engravings show the coat without the cape collars.

The mode is practical for cheviot, cloth, tweed, whipcord, covert cloth and many fancy suitings. The approved finish is machine-stitching.

Pattern 7830, *The Delineator,* **September 1895.**

1895 Costume

Illustration 104. Gray serge and white piqué were chosen for this costume for boys two to seven years old. Braid and buttons decorate it. The skirt is hemmed at the bottom, and the effect of a broad box plait is given in front by arrangement of the kilt plaits which turn from the front. The top of the skirt is finished with an under waistband in which buttonholes are made for attaching the skirt to the underwaist which is shaped with only shoulder seams and closed in front. The plain vest is closed at the back and is sufficiently deep in front to extend slightly over the skirt; it is decorated at the top of the front with an embroidered emblem.

The jaunty little middy jacket has a permanent and a removable sailor collar and is open in front all the way down. The back is nicely curved to the figure by side-back gores and a center seam. The fronts are reversed at the top by the permanent sailor collar which falls deep and square at the back and is overlapped by the removable collar of white piqué. The removable collar extends to the lower edge of the jacket fronts underneath and is made to underlap the back by a small fitted portion. The removable collar is attached to the jacket with buttonholes and buttons and is decorated with braid. The coat sleeves are finished at the wrists with a row of machine-stitching. The front edges of the jacket fronts and the outer folds of the box plait in the skirt are decorated with rows of buttons.

The suit may be appropriately made of cloth, serge, cheviot, tweed and so forth. The vest and removable collar may be of contrasting material.

The cap is of cloth.

Pattern No. 7817, *The Delineator,* **September 1895.**

50

1895 Costume

Illustration 105. White lawn, all-over embroidery, embroidered edging and plaid mohair are here combined in a costume for two to seven year olds. The plaid skirt, which is hemmed at the bottom, is arranged in kilt plaits all round and is finished with an under waistband by which it is attached to a sleeveless underwaist with buttons and buttonholes.

The blouse is fitted by the usual seams on the shoulders and under the arms. It displays a box plait at the center of the front; the lower edge is hemmed and drawn in closely about the waist by an elastic inserted in the hem, the blouse drooping in the customary style. The round ripple collar is deepened by a frill of embroidered edging which also extends up the front edges. A frill of narrower edging outlines the box plait which is overlaid with all-over embroidery. The shirt-sleeves are gathered at the top and bottom and are completed with rolling cuffs of all-over embroidery having frills of embroidered edging at the top.

The cap of light cloth consists of a band and a crown which extends in points beyond the head after the manner of a mortarboard cap. A silk tassel droops prettily to one side.

The blouse will usually be of silk lawn, nainsook or sheer cambric with all-over embroidery for the collar and cuffs and lace or embroidered edging for the frills. The skirt may be of piqué, serge, fancy cheviot or flannel.

Pattern Nos. 7810 (costume) and 4393 (cap), *The Delineator*, **September 1895.**

1896 Suit

Illustration 106. The combination of blue and white cloth here effected in the jaunty suit is attractively enhanced by the decoration of gilt braid and buttons. This costume is suitable for little boys from three to eight years of age. The middy vest is closed at the back. The jacket opens over the vest and is of uniform lower outline. Its deep sailor collar extends quite broadly upon the sleeves. A left breast pocket is finished with a welt.

The short trousers are closed at the sides and openings below the outside seams are closed with buttons and buttonholes.

To small boys there seems a great charm in suits that suggest the soldier or sailor. A nautical suit like this one made of blue and red or white flannel, serge or tweed will be made doubly attractive by a braid decoration and an appliqued anchor or other emblem on the vest.

Other developments will unite fawn and green, red and black or brown and white. Braid decorations are strongly adhered to for suits of this kind and emblems are appropriate adornments.

The cap is in sailor style.

Pattern No. 8614, *The Delineator,* **October 1896.**

Front View.

Back View.

1896 Jacket and Vest

Illustration 107. The middy vest and open jacket are attractive features of this suit in which navy blue and red flannel are here united. A variation of this suit is shown in *Illustration 106*

Pattern No. 8614, *The Delineator,* **October 1896.**

1896 Suit

Illustration 108. Wool diagonal was used for this stylish suit, the finish being given by stitching. The trousers, suitable for boys three to ten years of age, are of knee length and are closed at the sides.

The jacket, to be worn by three to eight year olds, has side and change pockets, the openings to which are finished with laps and a left breast pocket completed with a welt. The jacket is closed in double-breasted style. A rolling collar reverses the fronts in lapels above the closing and the side seams end above under laps allowed on the fronts. The sleeves are shapely and comfortable.

Suits like this are made of tweed, rough suitings in plain or mixed varieties, cheviot and other durable materials; braid and stitching are equally appropriate for finishing. Reefers are quite as often made up independently as they are to form parts of suits.

The derby hat is of correct shape.

Pattern No. 8615, *The Delineator,* **October 1896.**

Front View.   *Back View.*

1896 Reefer Jacket

Illustration 109. The material illustrated in this little boy's reefer jacket is rough mixed coating. This jacket is also shown in *Illustration 108.*

Pattern No. 8615, *The Delineator,* **October 1896.**

Front View.   *Back View.*

1896 Sack Coat

Illustration 110. A boy's three-button cutaway sack coat.

Pattern No. 8617, *The Delineator,* **October 1896.**

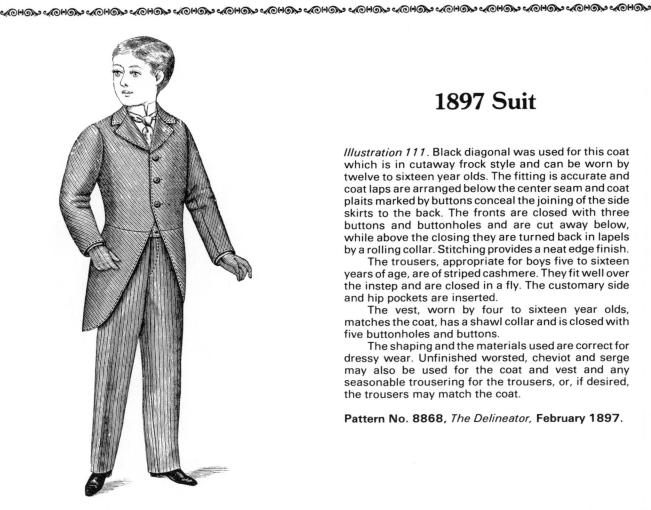

1897 Suit

Illustration 111. Black diagonal was used for this coat which is in cutaway frock style and can be worn by twelve to sixteen year olds. The fitting is accurate and coat laps are arranged below the center seam and coat plaits marked by buttons conceal the joining of the side skirts to the back. The fronts are closed with three buttons and buttonholes and are cut away below, while above the closing they are turned back in lapels by a rolling collar. Stitching provides a neat edge finish.

The trousers, appropriate for boys five to sixteen years of age, are of striped cashmere. They fit well over the instep and are closed in a fly. The customary side and hip pockets are inserted.

The vest, worn by four to sixteen year olds, matches the coat, has a shawl collar and is closed with five buttonholes and buttons.

The shaping and the materials used are correct for dressy wear. Unfinished worsted, cheviot and serge may also be used for the coat and vest and any seasonable trousering for the trousers, or, if desired, the trousers may match the coat.

Pattern No. 8868, *The Delineator,* **February 1897.**

1897 Coat

Illustration 112. The same coat as in *Illustration 111* is here pictured made of fine diagonal and finished with machine-stitching and buttons.

Pattern No. 8868, *The Delineator,* **February 1897.**

Front View.

Back View.

1897 Suit

Illustration 113. This is a natty suit that will please all little boys from three to ten years old. The coat is shown made of dark blue frieze; it is in box style. The back is seamless and the side seams are discontinued at the top of underlaps allowed on the fronts. A rolling collar reverses the fronts in lapels above the double-breasted closing which is made with buttons and buttonholes. The side pockets are provided with laps. Several rows of stitching outline round cuffs on the comfortable sleeves and three rows finish the other edges of the coat.

The trousers are of gray cloth. They extend to the knees and are closed at the sides.

The cap, which matches the trousers, is in Tam O'Shanter or sailor style and has a band that fits the head closely.

Heavy coatings such as chinchilla, beaver and rough mixtures are excellent for such coats. The trousers may be of any seasonable trousering and the cap may match either the coat or trousers.

Pattern Nos. 8867 (boy coat), 3163 (knee trousers) and 3033 (cap), *The Delineator,* **February 1897.**

1897 Middy Suit

Illustration 114. A combination of navy blue serge and white flannel is represented in this natty middy suit for boys from three to ten years of age. The blouse is drawn in to droop in the usual way by an elastic inserted in the hem at the bottom and is shaped in a V at the neck to disclose a buttoned-in shield ornamented with an embroidered emblem. A narrow standing collar finishes the shield and a deep sailor collar is added to the blouse, a tie being arranged in a sailor knot where the ends of the collar meet. A row of stitching is made near the edges of the sailor collar which falls over a smaller sailor collar on the jacket. The open fronts of the jacket are decorated with three large brass buttons. The coat-shaped sleeves are finished plainly.

The long sailor trousers are closed with a fly and show the regular nautical flare over the boots.

Most boys have a lively admiration for middy suits of cloth or flannel in red or blue combined with white and decorated with anchors, stars, chevrons and so forth.

The sailor cap of blue serge has the name of a cruiser embroidered on its band.

Pattern No. 8922, *The Delineator,* **March 1897.**

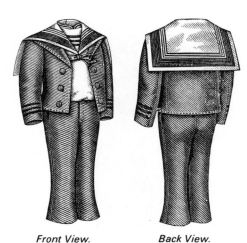

Front View.   Back View.

1897 Middy Suit

Illustration 115. The suit in the popular middy style is also shown in *Illustration 114.* Here it is developed in navy blue and red flannel.

Pattern No. 8922, *The Delineator,* **March 1897.**

1897 Vest

Illustration 116. This vest for boys ten to sixteen years old is particularly natty; it is pictured made of cloth and finished with machine-stitching. It is in three-button double-breasted style and is shaped by the customary center and side seams. The fronts are widened by gores joined so that the seams come at the center of the lap; peaked lapels are joined to the gores and covered with facings that are in sections. The lapels extend a little beyond the ends of the rolling collar. The width about the waist is regulated by the customary straps that start at the side seams and buckle at the back. Welts finish openings to a side pocket and a breast pocket inserted in each front.

The vest will be made of smooth-faced cloth matching or contrasting with the suit which it accompanies. For warm weather piqué or linen may be used, machine-stitching being all that is required in the way of completion.

Pattern No. 8985, *The Delineator,* **March 1897.**

1897 Coat

Illustration 117. The coat appropriate for young men ten to sixteen years old is illustrated made of diagonal and finished with machine-stitching. The fronts are closed with three buttons and buttonholes and are reversed above the closing in small pointed lapels that form notches with the well-shaped rolling collar. Below the closing the front edges of the coat fronts are rounded widely toward the back in the regular cutaway style. The back is nicely conformed to the figure by a center seam and is joined in side and shoulder seams to the fronts. A side pocket and a breast pocket in patch style are stitched on each front. The pockets have rounding lower edges and are finished at hem depth from the top with machine-stitching. The comfortable sleeves are shaped by the usual seams and are finished with roll-up cuffs of moderate depth. A row of stitching is made close to the edge on the cuffs, collar lapels and at the front edges, the latter stitching being continued about the lower edge of the coat.

Various suitings will be used for coats of this kind, rough goods, serge and cheviot being most popular.

Pattern No. 8986, *The Delineator,* **March 1897.**

 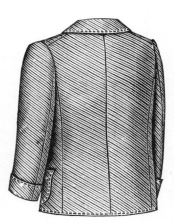

Front View.   Back View.

1897 Jacket and Blouse

Illustration 118. This blouse of fine lawn decorated with embroidered edging and jacket of velvet trimmed with braid are appropriate to wear with either trousers or kilts. To be worn by three to seven year olds, the blouse is shaped by shoulder and underarm seams and closed at the center of the front under a jabot of embroidered edging. The lower edge of the blouse is drawn closely about the waist by an elastic inserted in the hem, the blouse drooping in the customary manner. The full sleeves are finished with wristbands to which the roll-up cuffs are sewn, and a row of embroidered edging decorates the cuffs at the top. The deep round collar is mounted on a band and is finished with a frill of lawn that is bordered with a row of edging.

The jacket has a seamless back and is shaped by shoulder and underarm seams. The fronts open all the way down and the edges of the jacket are decorated with two rows of braid, the inner row being arranged in a fanciful pattern at the front edges. The cuffs of the blouse turn over the close sleeves of the jacket.

The jacket may be made of cloth, corduroy or velvet, dark shades of red, green, brown and blue being considered appropriate and becoming; the blouse will usually be made of lawn with embroidered edging for decoration.

Pattern No. 8988, *The Delineator,* **March 1897.**

Front View.

Back View.

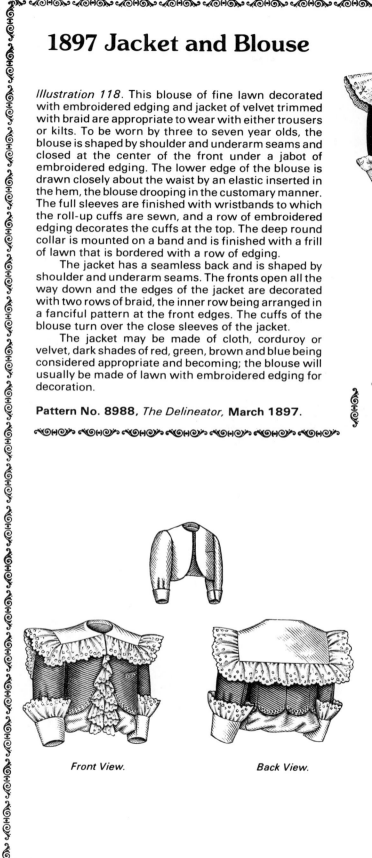

Front View.   *Back View.*

1897 Jacket and Blouse

Illustration 119. This blouse and jacket may be worn with either trousers or kilts by three to seven year olds. Lawn was selected for the blouse and dark red cloth for the jacket. The fronts and back of the blouse are joined in shoulder and underarm seams and the lower edge of the blouse is drawn closely to the waist by an elastic inserted in the hem, the blouse drooping in the regulation way. The deep sailor collar turns over from the top of a narrow band and its broad ends flare at the throat; it is bordered with a frill of edging. A double jabot of edging is arranged over the closing which is made with buttons and buttonholes at the center of the front. A frill of edging trims the top of the turn-up cuffs completing the sleeves which are gathered at the top and bottom.

The removable jacket is shaped with center, shoulder and side seams and is made short enough to show the blouse all round. The lower edge is scalloped at the back; the fronts, which open all the way, are rounded nicely toward the back. An opening to a breast pocket in the left front is finished with a welt. The sleeves are smooth fitting at the top and plaited at the bottom and are completed with straight cuffs that are hidden by the cuffs of the blouse. The blouse collar is adjusted over the jacket.

Nainsook or other sheer white goods will be used for dressy blouses with velvet or fine cloth for the jacket. For everyday wear chambray, figured lawn, cambric and so forth will be selected in conjunction with serge, flannel or, in warm weather, piqué.

Pattern No. 8989, *The Delineator,* **March 1897.**

1897 Coat

Front View.

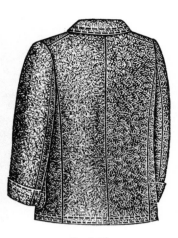

Back View.

Illustration 120. Fancy cheviot is illustrated in this stylish coat for boys from ten to sixteen years of age. The finish is machine-stitching. The collar rolls the fronts in pointed lapels above the closing which is made in double-breasted style with buttons and button-holes. The back is nicely conformed to the figure by a center seam and is joined in side and shoulder seams to the fronts. The comfortable sleeves are finished with round cuffs. Two side pockets and two breast pockets in patch style are stitched on the fronts.

The coat may be made of cheviot, tweed, rough or smooth cloth and fancy mixtures. The finish will usually be as illustrated.

Pattern No. 8987, *The Delineator,* **March 1897.**

1897 Middy Suit

Illustration 121. This jaunty middy suit will be a popular style for small boys, ages four to eight, during the coming season. It is pictured made of blue and red flannel with a finish of machine-stitching and a stylish decoration of braid and buttons. The middy vest is simply shaped by shoulder and side seams and closed at the back with buttons and buttonholes. A band finishes the neck.

The jacket is nicely conformed to the figure by side seams and a center seam and the fronts are closed on the breast with a hook and loop and flare above and below to reveal the vest. The sailor collar is broad and square across the back. Its pointed ends meet at the closing under a stylishly bowed silk tie. The fullness in the sleeve is disposed in shallow side plaits on the outside of the arm at the top and bottom, the plaits being stitched along their folds for a short distance. Openings to side pockets in the fronts are finished with welts.

The short trousers are shaped by the usual leg seams, center seam and hip darts. They are closed at the sides and the top is finished with underwaist bands in which buttonholes are made for attachment to the underwaist. The customary side pockets are conveniently inserted and buttons decorate the trousers near the lower edge just in front of the outside seams.

Serge, cloth, flannel and cheviot will be made up in this style and the vest will usually contrast with the remainder of the suit. Braid and machine-stitching will contribute the decoration. The jacket in this suit affords opportunity for the display of originality in the matter of decoration. Its smartly flaring fronts could be ornamented with narrow silk braid arranged in short cross rows or in various devices.

Pattern No. 8920, *The Delineator,* **March 1897.**

Front View.

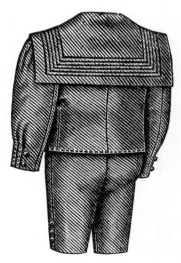

Back View.

1897 Sailor Suit

Illustration 122. The suit for three to ten year olds is in sailor style and is made up in a pretty combination of medium brown and cream white flannel. The lower edge of the blouse is drawn in about the waist on an elastic and the blouse is closed at the center of the front below the rounding ends of a large sailor collar that is decorated with a row of wide and narrow black braid. The removable shield is ornamented with an embroidered star and finished with a standing collar showing a line of narrow black braid at the edge. A bow is tacked over the ends of the sailor collar and a patch pocket is arranged on the left breast. The sleeves are plaited at the wrists and openings finished below the seams are closed with buttons and buttonholes.

The trousers reach just to the knees and are closed at the sides.

The suit has a jaunty air that is best shown when combinations of blue and white, red and white and so forth are arranged. Braid in one or several widths will always provide appropriate ornamentation.

Pattern No. 8923, *The Delineator,* **March 1897.**

Front View.   *Back View.*

1897 Sailor Suit

Illustration 123. This is another view of the boy's sailor blouse suit shown in *Illustration 122.* This time it is made of blue serge and red flannel and trimmed with braid, buttons, an embroidered emblem and machine-stitching. A satin tie and lanyard are worn.

Pattern No.8923, *The Delineator,* **March 1897.**

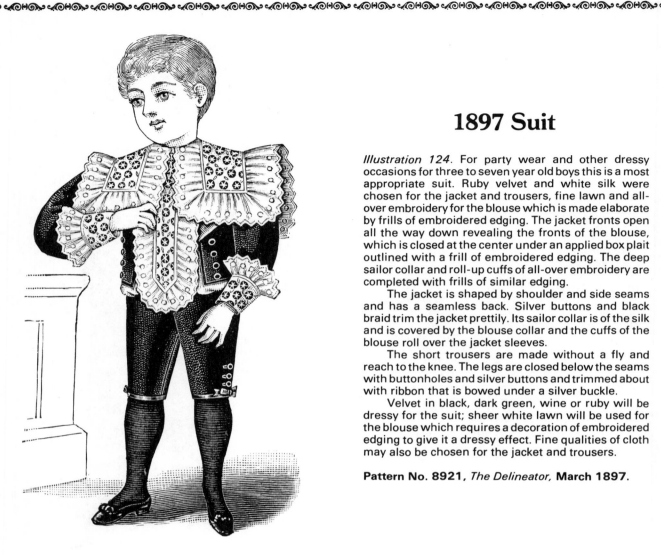

1897 Suit

Illustration 124. For party wear and other dressy occasions for three to seven year old boys this is a most appropriate suit. Ruby velvet and white silk were chosen for the jacket and trousers, fine lawn and all-over embroidery for the blouse which is made elaborate by frills of embroidered edging. The jacket fronts open all the way down revealing the fronts of the blouse, which is closed at the center under an applied box plait outlined with a frill of embroidered edging. The deep sailor collar and roll-up cuffs of all-over embroidery are completed with frills of similar edging.

The jacket is shaped by shoulder and side seams and has a seamless back. Silver buttons and black braid trim the jacket prettily. Its sailor collar is of the silk and is covered by the blouse collar and the cuffs of the blouse roll over the jacket sleeves.

The short trousers are made without a fly and reach to the knee. The legs are closed below the seams with buttonholes and silver buttons and trimmed about with ribbon that is bowed under a silver buckle.

Velvet in black, dark green, wine or ruby will be dressy for the suit; sheer white lawn will be used for the blouse which requires a decoration of embroidered edging to give it a dressy effect. Fine qualities of cloth may also be chosen for the jacket and trousers.

Pattern No. 8921, *The Delineator,* **March 1897.**

1897 Suit

Illustration 125. This suit, also shown in *Illustration 124,* is represented here made in dressy suit velvet, lawn, all-over embroidery, embroidered edging and insertion. It is handsomely combined with braid, fancy buckles and pearl buttons for decoration.

Pattern No. 8921, *The Delineator,* **March 1897.**

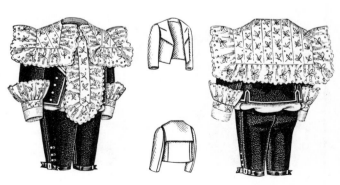

Front View.

Back View.

1897 Suit

Illustration 126. Military gray and cream flannel are united in this jaunty suit for four to eight year olds; gilt braid and buttons contribute effective decoration. The vest, which is closed at the back, has a rounding lower outline and is completed with a neck band.

The jacket is shaped by center, shoulder and side seams and the fronts are closed under a silk tie at the ends of the large sailor collar. Openings to pockets inserted in the fronts are finished with welts. The sleeves have fullness laid in plaits at the top and bottom.

The short trousers close at the sides and reach to the knee.

The suit will be made up in galatea, linen, serge, flannel and so forth; two colors of one material or a contrast of materials and colors will be in good taste. Braid and buttons will provide appropriate decoration. A very smart suit like this was made up of dark red cloth with the collar and vest of fawn cloth. Black and gilt braid and gilt buttons in two sizes were used in the decoration.

Pattern No. 8920, *The Delineator,* **March 1897.**

1897 Suit

Illustration 127. This jaunty costume of blue and white serge consists of short trousers without a fly and a sailor blouse having a removable sailor collar. It is to be worn by boys three to ten years of age. The blouse is drawn in on an elastic at the bottom and the fronts are cut low to accommodate the ends of a large sailor collar over which is arranged a smaller one of similar outline. The collars fall square at the back but are curved fancifully in front of the shoulders and a ribbon bow is set over the closing just below its ends. A shield disclosed in the open neck is decorated with an embroidered emblem and a patch pocket finished with a lap is applied on the left front. The comfortable sleeves are made with only inside seams and are finished with cuffs.

It has a matching cap.

Pattern No. 8994, *The Delineator,* **April 1897.**

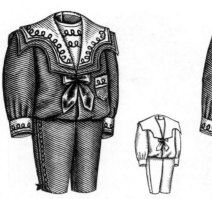

Front View.   *Back View.*

1897 Sailor Costume

Illustration 128. A sailor costume with short trousers without a fly. A different development can be seen in *Illustration 127.*

Pattern No. 8994, *The Delineator,* **April 1897.**

Front View.   *Back View.*

1897 Sailor Costume

Illustration 130. This sailor costume, also shown in *Illustration 129*, is here pictured made of blue serge with red serge for the vest; braid, buttons and an embroidered emblem provide the decoration.

Pattern No. 9020, *The Delineator,* **April 1897.**

1897 Suit

Illustration 129. Mixed cheviot, blue and white cloth and white silk form the combination here selected for the costume for three to ten-year-old boys. Braid, buttons and an embroidered emblem supply the decoration. The jaunty middy jacket has open fronts and a deep sailor collar. The sleeves are of comfortable width and square cornered laps cover the openings to side pockets in the fronts. The jacket opens over a navy vest of silk that has a full front showing a box plait at the center and is closed at the back. A broad belt finishes the lower edge of the front of the vest and a narrow band completes the neck. The trousers reach to the knees and are closed at the sides; buttons are set at the outside of the legs.

It has a matching hat appropriately decorated.

Pattern No. 9020, *The Delineator,* **April 1897.**

Front View.

Back View.

1897 Middy Jacket

Illustration 131. Blue serge and white flannel are combined in this natty middy jacket, the white flannel being used for the vest and also for the removable collar on the jacket. The vest is simply shaped by underarm and shoulder seams and closed at the back with buttonholes and buttons. The neck is finished with a band and an emblem is embroidered on the center of the front a little below the neck.

Underarm and shoulder seams perform the shaping of the jacket. The fronts are wide apart all the way and to them are joined the tapering ends of a large sailor collar that falls deep and square at the back and extends out upon the comfortable two-seam coat sleeves. Over this collar is arranged a somewhat smaller removable collar that buttons to the inside of the jacket and extends beneath the fronts to the lower edge. A cord looped over buttons sewn underneath to the removable collar connects the fronts of the jacket. Machine-stitching finishes the edges of the jacket and emblems are embroidered on the sleeves.

Jackets of the middy order are very stylish for general wear and also for outing, this one designed for three to ten-year-old boys. Flannels, serge and smooth cloth are the best woolens for them and duck and linen are used during the summer.

Pattern No. 8992, *The Delineator,* **April 1897.**

Front View.   *Back View.*

1897 Dress

Illustration 132. This dress is pictured made of linen and trimmed with edging. It is appropriate for one to four year old boys. The front and backs are joined in shoulder and short underarm seams and reach only to the waist at the sides where they are lengthened by skirt portions. In the front and back are arranged three box plaits. The closing is made at the back with a fly. At the neck is a turn down collar in two sections. The one-seam bishop sleeves are finished with wristbands. Straps of the material are tacked under the outer box plaits in front and buttoned at the back.

Pattern No. 8990, *The Delineator,* **April 1897.**

Front View.   *Back View.*

1897 Dress

Illustration 133. This dress for one to five year old boys is pictured made of gingham and trimmed with embroidery and buttons. The round body is fitted by shoulder and underarm seams and closed at the back. A tuck is taken up at each side of the center of the front and turned backward. Included in the shoulder and underarm seams are long jacket fronts; on each jacket front is a patch pocket. The sailor collar has short stole ends. The full sleeves are finished with wristbands. The full skirt has a double box plait laid at the center of the front. It is gathered at the top back of the box plait and joined to the body. Pointed straps crossed at the back are included in the underarm seams.

Pattern No. 8995, *The Delineator,* **April 1897.**

1897 Costume

Illustration 134. The skirt and jacket of this costume are made of piqué and the blouse of lawn with frills of edging for trimming. The skirt is arranged in wide box plaits all round and sewn to a sleeveless underwaist. This costume can be worn fashionably by two to five year old boys.

The blouse is shaped with shoulder and underarm seams and closed at the front. The lower edge is turned under to form a hem through which a tape or elastic is run and the blouse droops in the regulation style. The shirt-sleeves are finished with wristbands and round cuffs. The sailor collar, which is mounded on a neck band, has widely flaring ends.

The jacket is shaped by shoulder and underarm seams. Its fronts meet at the throat where they are closed invisibly. The coat sleeves are comfortably wide.

Pattern Nos. 8991 (costume) and 4393 (cap), *The Delineator,* **April 1897.**

1897 Costume

Illustration 135. This costume, also shown in *Illustration 134,* has the skirt and jacket made of piqué. The blouse is of lawn with frills of edging for trimming.

Pattern No. 8991, *The Delineator,* **April 1897.**

Front View.   *Back View.*

1897 Costume

Illustration 136. This costume for little boys from two to five years of age is made of brown mixed suiting and red serge. The skirt is laid in plaits turning from the center of the front giving the effect of a broad box plait. A belt having pointed ends closed with a button and buttonhole covers its joining to a sleeveless waist that is finished with a low standing collar.

The jacket is pointed at the center of the back and has pointed lower front covers. The fronts are apart all the way showing the waist front in vest effect. They are connected by a cord looped over buttons just below the ends of a large sailor collar. The sleeves are finished with round turn-up cuffs. A row of black braid trims the cuffs and sailor collar.

Cheviot, cloth, serge, duck, piqué, linen and so forth are all appropriate materials for costumes of this style. The effect is best when two colors or contrasting materials are combined. A simple trimming of braid will usually be added.

The sailor cap is made of the mixed suiting with a row of black braid over the band.

Pattern Nos. 9051 (costume) and 3033 (cap), *The Delineator,* **May 1897.**

Front View.   *Back View.*

1897 Costume

Illustration 137. The costume in *Illustration 136* is differently made here of blue and white striped linen combined with white piqué.

Pattern No. 9051, *The Delineator,* **May 1897.**

1897 Suit

Illustration 138. This handsome suit for three to eight year old boys is made up for dressy wear, the jacket and trousers being of black velvet with silk braid binding for the finish; the blouse is of fine white lawn with embroidered edging for the frills. A silk tie is bowed at the throat. The blouse is closed at the center of the front under an applied box plait that is outlined with frills of embroidered edging and the deep sailor collar and the roll-up cuffs are bordered with similar frills and arranged to fall over the jacket.

The simple shaping of the jacket is accomplished by center shoulder and side seams and the fronts are wide apart all the way showing the blouse front attractively.

The short trousers are shaped by the usual seams and are without a fly.

For dressy wear velvet, velveteen or corduroy in black or dark shades of garnet, ruby, green or purple will be effective with white nainsook or lawn for the blouse and embroidered edging for the blouse frills. When the suit is for everyday wear cloth, serge and some of the new cotton and linen fabrics may be selected with braid for ornamentation and the blouse may be of cambric.

The velvet cap has two quills caught under an ornament at the left side of the front.

Pattern No. 9054, *The Delineator,* **May 1897.**

Front View.

Back View.

1897 Costume

Illustration 139. Green fancy suiting and white piqué with embroidered edging for the frills form the stylish combination shown in this costume. Boys from two to five years of age will look well in this ensemble. The skirt, which is deeply hemmed at the bottom, is laid in box plaits all round and buttoned to a sleeveless underwaist that is shaped with shoulder and underarm seams and closed at the back.

The vest is fitted by shoulder and underarm seams and a center seam and is closed to the throat with buttons and buttonholes. Openings to side pockets in the fronts are finished with welts. Straps stitched to the back and fastened together with a buckle regulate the width at the waist. The neck is completed with a turn-down collar that has rounding front corners.

The jacket is shaped by center and side seams which are terminated a short distance above the lower edge to form the back in tabs; the fronts almost meet at the neck and flare sharply. The edges of the jacket are finished with machine-stitching. The large fancy collar and pointed cuffs, which are removable, are made of piqué and bordered with wide frills of embroidery; the collar is trimmed with rows of insertion arranged to flare toward the lower edge. The cuffs are mounted on bands that are turned under the close fitting sleeves. Pocket laps cover openings to side pockets in the fronts and a welt finishes a left breast pocket.

Mixed suiting, cheviot, serge, broadcloth and so forth combined with piqué and handsome embroidered edging will be appropriate for this little costume; silk braid and insertion will trim it daintily. In a very dressy suit brown velveteen and red silk were united, the silk being used for the vest, collars and cuffs. Pearl ball buttons were used for making the closing and fine Swiss embroidered edging contributed the frills. Insertions could have been arranged on the fancy collar as in the illustrations and the effect would have been especially dainty if the silk was cut away from beneath the insertion.

Pattern No. 9053, *The Delineator,* **May 1897.**

1897 Costume

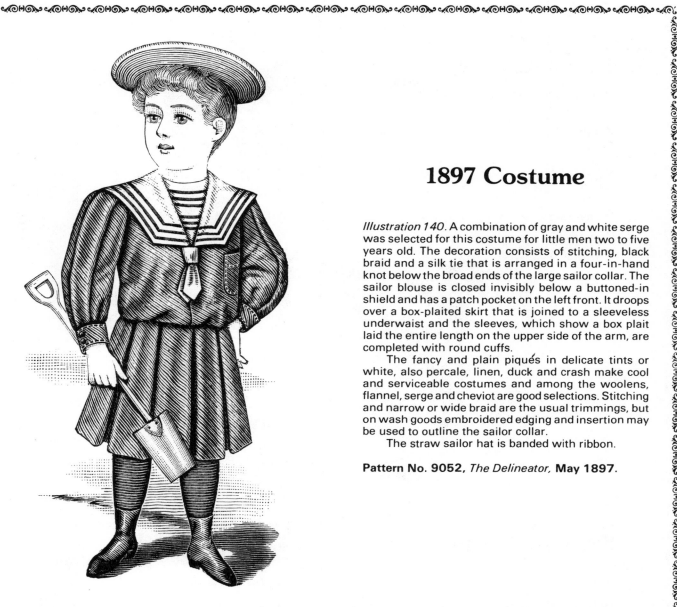

Illustration 140. A combination of gray and white serge was selected for this costume for little men two to five years old. The decoration consists of stitching, black braid and a silk tie that is arranged in a four-in-hand knot below the broad ends of the large sailor collar. The sailor blouse is closed invisibly below a buttoned-in shield and has a patch pocket on the left front. It droops over a box-plaited skirt that is joined to a sleeveless underwaist and the sleeves, which show a box plait laid the entire length on the upper side of the arm, are completed with round cuffs.

The fancy and plain piqués in delicate tints or white, also percale, linen, duck and crash make cool and serviceable costumes and among the woolens, flannel, serge and cheviot are good selections. Stitching and narrow or wide braid are the usual trimmings, but on wash goods embroidered edging and insertion may be used to outline the sailor collar.

The straw sailor hat is banded with ribbon.

Pattern No. 9052, *The Delineator,* **May 1897.**

1897 Costume

Illustration 141. This practical and becoming costume, also shown in *Illustration 140*, is developed this time in blue and white flannel and finished with machine-stitching.

Pattern No. 9052, *The Delineator,* **May 1897.**

Front View.   Back View.

Front View.

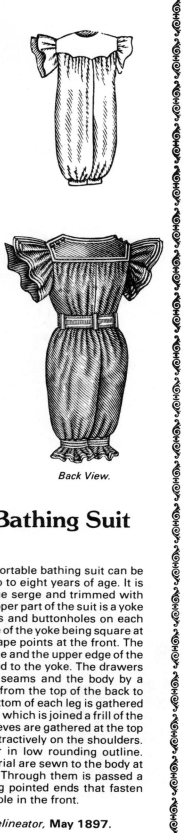

Back View.

1897 Child Bathing Suit

Illustration 142. This comfortable bathing suit can be worn by children from two to eight years of age. It is pictured made of navy blue serge and trimmed with narrow white braid. The upper part of the suit is a yoke that is closed with buttons and buttonholes on each shoulder, the lower outline of the yoke being square at the back and curved to shape points at the front. The body and drawers are in one and the upper edge of the body is gathered and joined to the yoke. The drawers are shaped by inside leg seams and the body by a center seam that extends from the top of the back to the top of the front. The bottom of each leg is gathered and finished with a band to which is joined a frill of the material. The short full sleeves are gathered at the top and their ends separate attractively on the shoulders. The neck may be high or in low rounding outline. Narrow straps of the material are sewn to the body at intervals about the waist. Through them is passed a belt of the material having pointed ends that fasten with a button and buttonhole in the front.

Pattern No. 9114, *The Delineator,* **May 1897.**

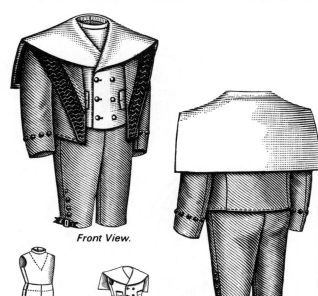

Front View.

Back View.

1897 Suit

Illustration 143. This suit, consisting of a jacket with sailor collar, a double-breasted vest with sailor collar and trousers without a fly is appropriate for boys from four to eight years of age. It is illustrated made of cloth and the vest of white duck. The jacket is simply shaped by underarm and shoulder seams. The fronts are wide apart all the way down. The sailor collar extends to the bottom of the jacket fronts, its ends tapering gradually and is covered at the back by a larger sailor collar on the vest. The comfortable sleeves are decorated at cuff depth with an encircling row of buttons. Braid on the collar and a row of stitching at the lower edge finish the jacket stylishly.

The trousers are without a fly and are shaped by the usual seams. They are buttoned to a sleeveless underwaist that is closed at the back. A facing of white duck is applied on the front of the underwaist and the neck is completed with a narrow band. A ribbon bow with a buckle and a row of three buttons decorate each leg at the outside seam.

The fronts of the vest are joined in shoulder and side seams to the back, which is shaped by a curved center seam. The customary straps on the back regulate the width about the waist. The vest is closed in double-breasted style with buttons and buttonholes. The neck is shaped low in front, revealing the facing on the underwaist in shield effect. The sailor collar laps with the fronts and has tapering ends. Openings to inserted pockets are covered with square-cornered laps that are stitched across the center.

Piqué, duck and fancy vesting may be chosen for the vest and cloth, serge, flannel, cheviot and some of the cool summer suitings like galatea or linen will be selected for the jacket and trousers.

Pattern No. 9120, *The Delineator,* **June 1897.**

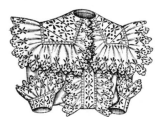

Front View.   Back View.

1897 Blouse

Illustration 144. A blouse for little boys two to eight years of age is here depicted made of white nainsook, all-over embroidery and embroidered edging. It is shaped by shoulder and underarm seams and closed at the center of the front under an applied plait of the all-over embroidery bordered at each side by a frill of the embroidered edging. The lower edge of the blouse is hemmed to hold an elastic that draws the edge closely about the waist, the blouse drooping in the customary way. The lower outline of the deep sailor collar is gracefully curved to form a point at the center of the back and the ends flare from the throat; the collar is mounted on a band and bordered with a frill of the edging. Pointed cuffs made to accord with the collar are turned up over narrow bands and prettily complete the full sleeves. A narrow band covers the joinings of the frills.

The blouse may be made of lawn, nainsook, cambric, dimity or batiste and decorated with lace edging.

Pattern No. 9140, *The Delineator,* **June 1897.**

1897 Middy Suit

Illustration 145. Blue and white serge are united in this handsome middy suit suitable for five to ten-year-old boys. The decoration is provided by blue braid, an embroidered emblem on the vest, gilt buttons and machine-stitching. An unusually large sailor collar on the shapely jacket laps with the fronts which close in a double-breasted style and in the open neck a vest is revealed in shield effect. The vest is finished with a neck band and is closed at the back.

The trousers, which are made with a fly, are long and flare over the boot in correct sailor style.

These popular suits are made of flannel or cloth in red, brown or cadet gray or blue combined with white piqué, linen duck or galatea and trimmed with braid and buttons. A suit of cadet gray serge may have a sailor collar of white bengaline. The vest may match the collar.

The sailor cap of white serge has the name of some well known ship embroidered on its band.

Pattern No. 9119, *The Delineator,* **June 1897.**

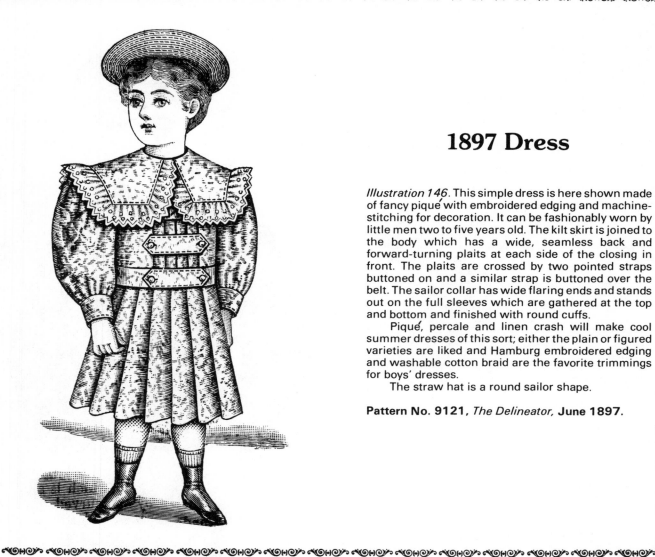

1897 Dress

Illustration 146. This simple dress is here shown made of fancy piqué with embroidered edging and machine-stitching for decoration. It can be fashionably worn by little men two to five years old. The kilt skirt is joined to the body which has a wide, seamless back and forward-turning plaits at each side of the closing in front. The plaits are crossed by two pointed straps buttoned on and a similar strap is buttoned over the belt. The sailor collar has wide flaring ends and stands out on the full sleeves which are gathered at the top and bottom and finished with round cuffs.

Piqué, percale and linen crash will make cool summer dresses of this sort; either the plain or figured varieties are liked and Hamburg embroidered edging and washable cotton braid are the favorite trimmings for boys' dresses.

The straw hat is a round sailor shape.

Pattern No. 9121, *The Delineator,* **June 1897.**

1897 Dress

Illustration 147. This dress is differently portrayed in *Illustration 146.* White piqué was chosen for this natty little dress. The skirt is laid in kilt plaits all round and joined to the body which has a seamless back that is separated from the fronts by wide underarm gores. The closing is made invisibly at the center between forward-turning plaits laid in the fronts. A belt of the material covers the joining of the skirt and body and two pointed straps are buttoned across the plaits and one on the belt, the effect being quite ornamental. The full sleeves are gathered at the top and bottom and finished with round cuffs. At the neck is a broad sailor collar that falls deep and square at the back and has wide flaring ends; it is bordered with a frill of edging.

Piqué, linen, wash cheviot, serge and wool suiting will make up satisfactorily in this style with a trimming of embroidered edging and fancy braid.

Pattern No. 9121, *The Delineator,* **June 1897.**

Front View.

Back View.

Front View.   Back View.

1897 Costume

Illustration 148. This attractive costume, designated as the "Commodore costume," can be worn by boys from two to five years of age. It is shown made of linen in combination with white piqué. Machine-stitching provides the finish.

The skirt is laid in kilt plaits all round and may be buttoned or stitched to a sleeveless waist shaped by shoulder and underarm seams and closed at the back. The neck of the waist is completed with a neck band.

The back of the jacket displays a pointed lower outline and is shaped by shoulder and side back seams and a well-curved center seam. The fronts open all the way down and display between them the waist front which is of white piqué. They are connected by a chain or cord slipped over buttons sewn on the fronts below the sailor collar. The collar falls deep and square at the back and has wide fancifully curved ends. The collar combines the two materials and the edge of the piqué is piped. A belt of the material with pointed ends is closed in front with two buttons and buttonholes. The coat sleeves have pointed turn-up cuffs.

Linen and cotton duck, linen crash, cheviot, serge, cloth and flannel are used for costumes of this style and braid will be a satisfactory trimming.

Pattern No. 9118, *The Delineator,* **June 1897.**

1897 Dress

Illustration 149. This dress, to be worn by boys from two to five year old, is shown made of blue and white serge. Braid decorates it simply, but effectively. The front is laid in a box plait at each side of the center and the closing is made at the back. The double collar is exceedingly stylish and the full sleeves are finished with roll-up cuffs. The skirt is hemmed at the bottom and laid in kilt plaits that are turned toward the back, producing the effect of a broad box plait at the center of the front. The skirt is joined to the lower edge of the body. The belt has a pointed overlapping end and is closed in front.

The little dress will make up in cool fabrics like gingham, linen and Russian crash for warm weather. For cool weather serge, flannel and cheviot are always durable and neat.

The straw hat has a ribbon binding on its wide brim and a band of ribbon about its crown.

Pattern No. 9172, *The Delineator,* **July 1897.**

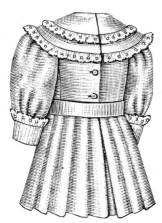

1897 Dress

Illustration 150. This boyish dress is here illustrated made of white piqué and trimmed with embroidered edging and insertion. The same dress appears in *Illustration 149*.

Pattern No. 9172, *The Delineator,* **July 1897.**

Front View.   Back View.

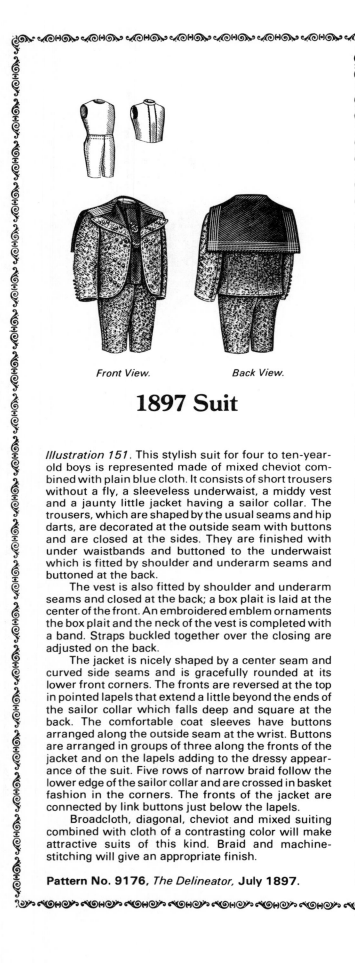

Front View.   *Back View.*

1897 Suit

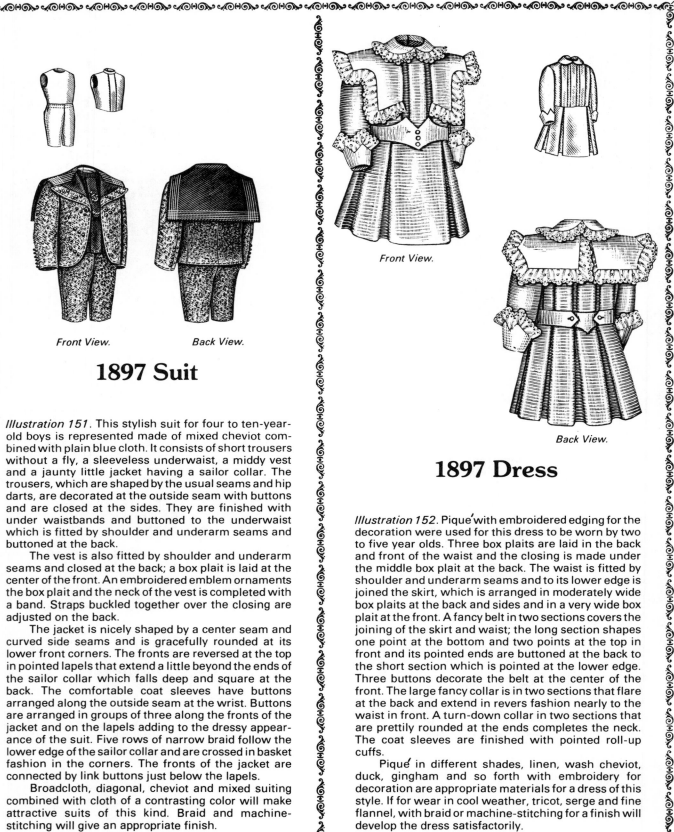

Front View.

Back View.

1897 Dress

Illustration 151. This stylish suit for four to ten-year-old boys is represented made of mixed cheviot combined with plain blue cloth. It consists of short trousers without a fly, a sleeveless underwaist, a middy vest and a jaunty little jacket having a sailor collar. The trousers, which are shaped by the usual seams and hip darts, are decorated at the outside seam with buttons and are closed at the sides. They are finished with under waistbands and buttoned to the underwaist which is fitted by shoulder and underarm seams and buttoned at the back.

The vest is also fitted by shoulder and underarm seams and closed at the back; a box plait is laid at the center of the front. An embroidered emblem ornaments the box plait and the neck of the vest is completed with a band. Straps buckled together over the closing are adjusted on the back.

The jacket is nicely shaped by a center seam and curved side seams and is gracefully rounded at its lower front corners. The fronts are reversed at the top in pointed lapels that extend a little beyond the ends of the sailor collar which falls deep and square at the back. The comfortable coat sleeves have buttons arranged along the outside seam at the wrist. Buttons are arranged in groups of three along the fronts of the jacket and on the lapels adding to the dressy appearance of the suit. Five rows of narrow braid follow the lower edge of the sailor collar and are crossed in basket fashion in the corners. The fronts of the jacket are connected by link buttons just below the lapels.

Broadcloth, diagonal, cheviot and mixed suiting combined with cloth of a contrasting color will make attractive suits of this kind. Braid and machine-stitching will give an appropriate finish.

Pattern No. 9176, *The Delineator,* **July 1897.**

Illustration 152. Piqué with embroidered edging for the decoration were used for this dress to be worn by two to five year olds. Three box plaits are laid in the back and front of the waist and the closing is made under the middle box plait at the back. The waist is fitted by shoulder and underarm seams and to its lower edge is joined the skirt, which is arranged in moderately wide box plaits at the back and sides and in a very wide box plait at the front. A fancy belt in two sections covers the joining of the skirt and waist; the long section shapes one point at the bottom and two points at the top in front and its pointed ends are buttoned at the back to the short section which is pointed at the lower edge. Three buttons decorate the belt at the center of the front. The large fancy collar is in two sections that flare at the back and extend in revers fashion nearly to the waist in front. A turn-down collar in two sections that are prettily rounded at the ends completes the neck. The coat sleeves are finished with pointed roll-up cuffs.

Piqué in different shades, linen, wash cheviot, duck, gingham and so forth with embroidery for decoration are appropriate materials for a dress of this style. If for wear in cool weather, tricot, serge and fine flannel, with braid or machine-stitching for a finish will develop the dress satisfactorily.

Pattern No. 9173, *The Delineator,* **July 1897.**

1897 Sailor Suit

Illustration 153. This natty sailor suit is made of blue and white flannel and trimmed with narrow braid. It is designed to be worn by three to ten-year-old boys. The fronts and back of the blouse are jointed in shoulder and underarm seams and an elastic or tape is inserted in a hem at the lower edge to draw the edge close to the waist, the blouse drooping in the customary sailor blouse style. The neck is shaped low in front, revealing a shield that is buttoned to the blouse and closed at the back. The shield is decorated with an embroidered emblem and finished at the neck with a band. The blouse is finished with a large sailor collar that falls deep and square at the back. The one-seam sleeve has fullness at the bottom disposed in three forward-turning plaits that are stitched along their folds to cuff depth; it is closed at the back of the wrist with buttons and buttonholes. Stitching finishes the opening to a breast pocket inserted in the left front. A black satin Windsor tie is knotted just below the ends of the collar.

The short trousers are shaped by the usual seams and hip darts. They are closed at the sides and are buttoned to a sleeveless underwaist that is fitted by shoulder and underarm seams and closed at the back.

Serge, cloth, flannel and cheviot will be made up in this style and the collar and shield will usually contrast with the remainder of the suit. Braid and machine-stitching will contribute to the decoration.

Pattern No. 9177, *The Delineator,* **July 1897.**

Front View.   *Back View.*

1897 Dress

Illustration 154. Red striped linen and plain white lawn are united in this natty dress for two to five-year-old boys. The pretty decoration is arranged with embroidered edging, white washable braid and pearl buttons. The skirt is laid in a very wide box plait at the center of the front and in moderately wide box plaits the rest of the way; it is joined to the body which shows three box plaits at both the front and back, the middle plait at the back concealing the closing. The fancy collar flares at the closing and extends in revers fashion down each side of the front. A plaid silk bow is seen between the ends of the turn-down collar. Pointed cuffs turn up from the wrists of the sleeves and the belt, being of fancy outline, is quite an ornamental adjunct.

Piqué, crash, duck and cotton cheviot will give satisfaction made up like this and lawn would combine prettily with any of these. Wash braids and embroidered edging and insertion are the best decorations. Pipings of white are effective on dresses in tan or bright colors.

The hat is a straw sailor.

Pattern No. 9173, *The Delineator,* **July 1897.**

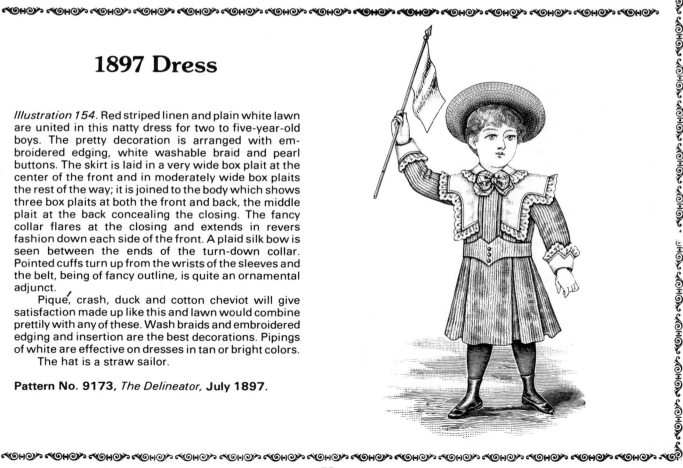

1897 Shirtwaist

Front View.

Illustration 155. This simple and comfortable shirtwaist is made of white cambric. It can be worn by boys from four to fourteen years of age. The fronts and seamless back, which are joined in shoulder and underarm seams, are smooth at the top, but have fullness below collected in two rows of gatherings at the waist both back and front, the gatherings being concealed beneath an applied belt. The closing is made with buttonholes and buttons through a box plait applied on the left front. Buttons are sewn on the belt for the attachment of the skirt or trousers. The neck may be finished with a turn-down collar that is mounted on a fitted band, or with a standing collar having bent corners. A Windsor tie is invariably worn with the turn-down collar. The shirt sleeves are gathered at the top and bottom and finished in the regular way with underlaps and pointed overlaps.

Percale, linen, cambric and gingham are favored for shirtwaists of this kind.

Pattern No. 9174, *The Delineator,* **July 1897.**

Back View.

1897 Box Coat

Front View.

Back View.

Illustration 156. Dark blue cloth was selected for this box coat and machine-stitching provides the finish. The broad, seamless back is jointed to the double-breasted fronts by shoulder and side seams. The fronts are rolled in pointed lapels and are closed in double-breasted style with buttons and buttonholes just below the lapels and in a fly below. The lapels form narrow notches with the rolling coat collar. The comfortable coat sleeves are shaped by the usual seams and the square cornered pocket laps cover openings to side pockets inserted in the fronts.

This box coat for three to eight-year-old boys is appropriate for wear over sailor blouses and so forth; it may be developed satisfactorily in kersey, melton or broadcloth.

Pattern No. 9175, *The Delineator,* **July 1897.**

Front View.   **Back View.**

1897 Costume

Illustration 158. This exceptionally pretty costume for a little boy, also shown in *Illustration 157*, is illustrated made of blue serge in combination with white serge.

Pattern No. 9227, *The Delineator,* **August 1897.**

Front View.   **Back View.**

1897 Costume

Illustration 159. The jaunty and comfortable costume for boys from two to five years of age is illustrated made of blue serge with red serge for the collar and cuffs. The skirt is hemmed at the bottom and laid in kilt plaits that turn toward the center of the back to produce the effect of a broad box plait at the center of the front. It is joined to a high-necked sleeveless underwaist that is shaped with shoulder and underarm seams and closed at the back.

The fronts and back of the blouse are joined in shoulder and underarm seams and an elastic or tape is inserted in a hem at the lower edge to draw the edge in about the waist and make the blouse droop in the customary way. The closing is made at the center of the front with buttons and buttonholes or with studs through a side box plait that is applied to the left front. The collar is deep and round and its ends flare from the throat. The bishop sleeves are gathered at the top and bottom and completed with roll-over pointed cuffs. Several rows of narrow blue braid decorate the collar and cuffs.

Duck, piqué, serge, cheviot, galatea, linen and flannel are suitable for a costume of this style. Braid in several widths, machine-stitching and fancy buttons will supply the decoration.

Pattern No. 9224, *The Delineator,* **August 1897.**

1897 Russian Costume

Illustration 157. The picturesque Russian costume shown here is made of red serge and decorated with white braid. It is fashionable for boys two to five years of age. A white silk tie is bowed between the ends of the large sailor collar which are rounded at the throat. The blouse droops in the regulation manner. The front is gathered at the neck and the closing is made in Russian style at the right side of the front through an overlap that is pointed at the lower end. The full sleeves are plaited to cuff depth, the plaits being stitched to position. The kilt skirt is joined in a high necked, sleeveless waist.

The costume is appropriate for duck, linen crash and piqué as for flannel, serge and smooth cloth. Braid is the most desirable trimming on all except piqué.

The tam cap is banded by a ribbon on which a ship's name is printed in gilt letters.

Pattern No. 9227, *The Delineator,* **August 1897.**

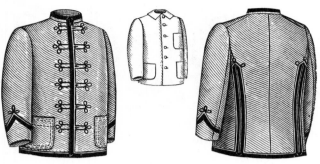

Front View.   *Back View.*

1897 Jacket

Illustration 160. Dark gray cloth was chosen for this jaunty uniform or cycling jacket; black braid provides a stylish military decoration. At the back and sides the jacket is gracefully conformed to the figure by side back gores and a curving center seam; the loose fronts are closed to the throat with buttons and buttonholes, the braid being applied on the front to simulate frogs. The coat sleeve is shaped by the usual seams at the inside and outside of the arm and the braid is arranged at the wrist to simulate pointed cuffs. A side pocket is applied to each front and a breast pocket to the left front; the breast pocket may be omitted. The neck may be completed with a standing collar or with a turn down collar having flaring ends.

This style jacket is appropriate for wear when a uniform is needed and is a most comfortable garment for cycling and kindred sports.

Pattern No. 1413, *The Delineator,* **August 1897.**

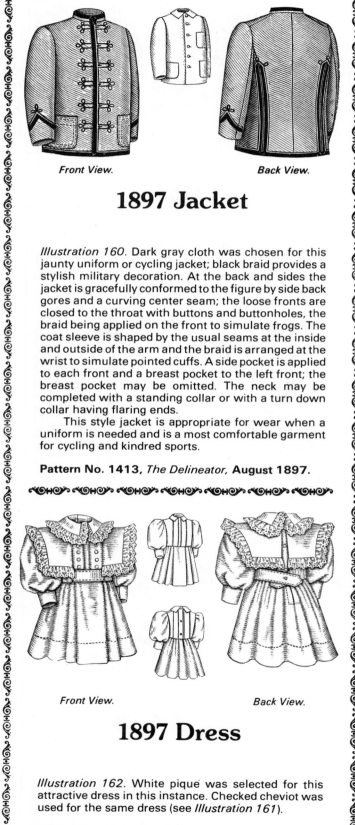

Front View.   *Back View.*

1897 Dress

Illustration 162. White piqué was selected for this attractive dress in this instance. Checked cheviot was used for the same dress (see *Illustration 161*).

Pattern No. 9226, *The Delineator,* **August 1897.**

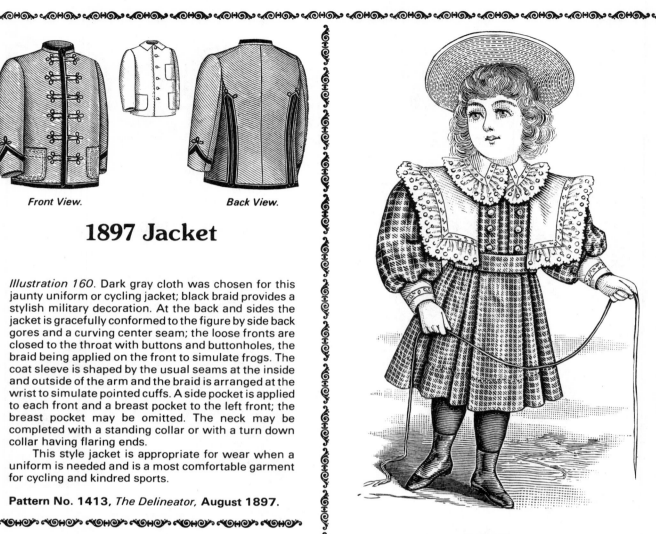

1897 Dress

Illustration 161. Checked cheviot is here pictured in a dress with white piqué for the collar and wristbands and insertion, buttons and embroidered edging for decoration. It is suitable for little boys from two to five years of age. The skirt is formed in a double box plait at the center of the front and gathered back of the plait; it is joined to the waist which is closed at the back. The waist is box plaited at the front and back and a belt passed through straps of the material has its ends crossed at the back. The full-gathered sleeves are completed with wristbands and the large stole sailor collar in two sections falls deep and square at the back and frames the box plaits in the front. The neck is finished with a rolling collar, the ends of which flare at the front and back.

Little dresses like this will be made of such goods as galatea, wash cheviot, linen, gingham and piqué, while serviceable heavier dresses will be of serge, flannel and cheviot with piqué or lawn for the collars and wristbands.

The broad-brimmed sailor hat is of white straw.

Pattern No. 9226, *The Delineator,* **August 1897.**

Front View.   *Back View.*

1897 Overcoat

Illustration 163. This stylish overcoat for two to five-year-old boys is pictured made of brown cloth with a handsome collar of light tan cloth bordered with a frill of edging. The seamless back is laid in two box plaits at the center and is separated from the fronts by underarm gores. The fronts lap diagonally from the throat to the waist, below which the lap is wide and straight. They are closed invisibly. A stylish accessory is the collar which falls deep and square at the back and has tapering ends that are joined to the front edges of the fronts of the waist and lapped in shawl fashion. A belt surrounds the waist and closes in front with a fancy buckle. The one-seam sleeves have gathered fullness at the top and fit the arm closely below the elbow.

Two shades of cloth are frequently used for coats of this style; one material may be used if preferred. Decoration consisting of bands of fur, braid or velvet may be applied with good effect.

Pattern No. 9279, *The Delineator,* **September 1897.**

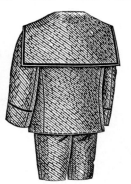

Front View.   *Back View.*

1897 Suit

Illustration 165. This is the same suit as shown in *Illustration 164.* Here it is made of cheviot and decorated with braid put on as a binding on the collar and in cuff outline on the comfortable sleeves.

Pattern No. 9277, *The Delineator,* **September 1897.**

1897 Suit

Illustration 164. Blue serge was used for this stylish suit for four to ten-year-old boys. It is finished with stitching and buttons. The reefer is seamless at the back and its loose fronts are closed in double-breasted style with buttonholes and bone buttons. Above the closing the fronts are reversed in pointed lapels that flare slightly from the ends of a deep square sailor collar. The sleeves are of comfortable width. Laps finish openings to a breast, change and side pockets. The short trousers are made without a fly and close at the sides.

The cap, a jaunty sailor or Tam-O'Shanter style, is made of material matching the suit.

Very natty suits can be made like this of brown, black or blue cheviot, serge or smooth cloth. Braid is as much liked as stitching for a finish and gilt buttons will give a bright effect.

Pattern No. 9277, *The Delineator,* **September 1897.**

1897 Overcoat

Illustration 166. This handsome overcoat is made of plaid cloth and is known as the Claude Duval or highwayman topcoat. Its double-breasted fronts are closed with buttonholes and bone buttons and are reversed in pointed lapels by a rolling collar which meets the lapels in notches. A stylish feature of the overcoat is the triple cape which is attached underneath the collar with hooks and eyes. The back clings gracefully to the form and displays coat laps and coat plaits; the sleeves are completed with round turn-up cuffs. Square cornered pocket laps cover openings to inserted pockets.

The leggings are of plain cloth and fit closely; they may extend to the thigh or be in medium or short length and are finished with stitching.

The coat will be made of plain or fancy coating and finished with braid or stitching. A handsome overcoat may be made of dark green broadcloth with pearl buttons for closing and decorating the cuffs. The leggings may be cut from the same material as the overcoat.

The cap matches the overcoat.

Pattern No. 9274 (overcoat) and 3475 (leggings), *The Delineator,* **September 1897.**

1897 Overcoat

Illustration 167. The overcoat with the triple cape is here shown again, this time made of diagonal with machine-stitching and buttons for completion. See *Illustration 166* for a variation of this overcoat. Heavy qualities of cloth like beaver, melton, thibet and so forth will be chosen for the coat if it is intended for the coldest season and cheviot, whipcord, tweed or cloth for the intermediate seasons.

Pattern No. 9274, *The Delineator,* **September 1897.**

Front View.   *Back View.*

1897 Coat

Front View.

Back View.

Illustration 168. This practical and stylish coat will meet with much favor during the coming season for boys two to five years of age. Gray cloth of fine quality was selected for its development and braid outlines the collar, cape and cuffs and is arranged in a trefoil design at the top of each opening in the cape. The short body is shaped by shoulder and underarm seams and closed at the center of the front with buttonholes and buttons. To it is joined the full skirt which is laid in three box plaits at the back and gathered in front of the plaits. A belt conceals the joining of the skirt and body and is slipped through straps at the sides and fastened in front with a fancy buckle. The stylish cape slashed to form oddly shaped tabs almost conceals the body and a rolling collar with flaring ends completes the neck. The full sleeves are gathered at the top and bottom and are fancifully shaped; roll-up cuffs complete them.

For autumn wear the coat will be made of cloth, cheviot, tweed and fancy coating trimmed with braid and for the colder days heavier coatings will be chosen and fur or velvet will form the decoration.

Pattern No. 9276, *The Delineator,* **September 1897.**

1897 Suit

Illustration 169. This stylish suit for boy three to eight years of age is pictured made of blue and red serge and decorated with braid and machine-stitching. The blouse is shaped by shoulder and underarm seams and closed at the right side of the front where an opening is made to a convenient depth and finished with a pointed overlap. The back is smooth at the top but the front has fullness gathered at the neck; the blouse is held in about the waist by a belt with pointed ends that fastens with a buckle at the right side of the front. The large sailor collar falls deep and square at the back and its broad ends flare prettily from the throat. The fullness in the sleeves is collected in gathers at the top and in tiny plaits at the wrists, the plaits being stitched along their outer folds.

The shaping of the trousers is accomplished by the customary seams and hip darts and the closing is made at the sides. The legs are turned under at the lower edges for hems in which elastic is inserted to draw the edges closely about the knee, the fullness drooping in Turkish fashion. The top of the trousers is finished in the usual way with waistbands stitched underneath and buttonholes are made in the waistbands for the attachment of the sleeveless underwaist which is closed at the back.

Little suits of this style will be made up in a combination of red and blue flannel or serge, or in cheviot, tweed or cloth of any admired color or mixture of colors. Braid and machine-stitching will provide the decorative finish.

Pattern No. 9275, *The Delineator,* **September 1897.**

Front View.

Back View.

1897 Coat

Illustration 170. The jaunty coat or jacket is made of green mixed cheviot with braid for a finish, and the kilt of a bright clan plaid. Two to six year old boys will find this suit desirable. The plaits in the kilt all turn toward the back, thus producing a broad box plait at the front, but the kilt may be kilt plaited all round if preferred.

The coat or jacket is gracefully fitted at the back and is closed in double-breasted style to the throat with buttonholes and buttons, the fronts being cut away stylishly below the closing. A sailor collar with broad ends falls deep and square at the back. Pocket laps with rounding lower front corners cover openings to inserted side pockets while a breast pocket opening in the left front is completed with a binding. The sleeves are comfortably made and are shaped with inside and outside seams; a round cuff is outlined on each with a row of braid. Braid forms a neat finish.

Little boys will be delighted with this suit which will be made up in combinations of clan plaids with red, brown or green cloth. The coat will usually be of serge, whipcord, suiting or cloth in any seasonable weight. Braid is the favored finish but machine-stitching is always liked. Checked, striped and plaid wool goods will be selected for the kilt and the cap may match either the coat or the kilt.

The green cloth Scotch cap pictured here is decorated with quills and a buckle.

Pattern No. 9278, *The Delineator,* **September 1897.**

Front View.

Back View.

1897 Jacket

Illustration 171. The jacket previously shown in *Illustration 170* is pictured here made of mixed cheviot and decorated with braid put on as a binding on the collar and in cuff outline on the sleeves.

Pattern No. 9278, *The Delineator,* **September 1897.**

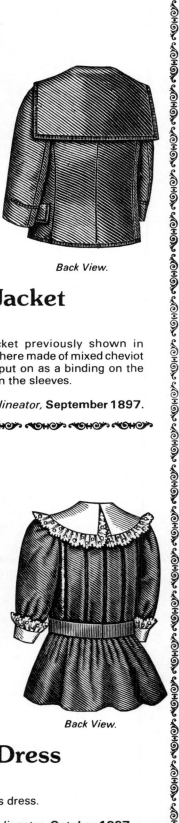

Front View.

Back View.

1897 Dress

Illustration 172. Little boy's dress.

Pattern No. 9346, *The Delineator,* **October 1897.**

1897 Overcoat

Illustration 173. This is a pleasing style of long coat or overcoat for little boys from two to five years old. Dark green cloth was here chosen for it. The loose fronts close to the throat in double-breasted style with buttonholes and large pearl buttons; the back is laid in a double box plait at the center and hangs from a square yoke. A broad square sailor collar with stole ends give a dressy touch; it is bordered with chinchilla which also covers the low standing collar and follows the upper edge of fancy turn-up cuffs completing the coat sleeves.

The Tam O'Shanter cap matches the coat and is decorated with quill feathers fastened under a button at the left side.

Velvet or corded silk would make a handsome coat of this style and such materials as wide-wale English serge, cheviot, faced cloth or homespun in shades of navy, tan, green and so forth could be made dressy by braiding plainly or fancifully applied, or fur bands. Heavy lace and fur are suitable trimmings for the first-mentioned materials. The cap will sometimes be of the coat fabric and braid; rosettes and feathers are favored for decorating it. A handsome overcoat for a little man was made of dark red melton. Large white pearl buttons were used for closing and also for ornament and beaver fur was applied over the collar and cuffs.

Pattern No. 9347 (overcoat) and 845 (cap), *The Delineator,* **October 1897.**

1897 Coat

Illustration 174. Light gray bengaline silk was chosen for this dressy little coat, also seen in *Illustration 173*.

Pattern No. 9347, *The Delineator,* **October 1897.**

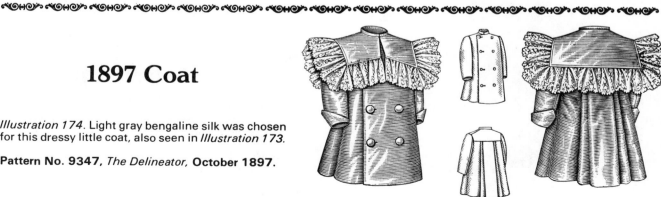

Front View. *Back View.*

1897 Overcoat

Illustration 175. A handsome quality of diagonal was selected for this overcoat which is in sack style and designed to be worn by boys from five to sixteen years of age. The back is shaped by a center seam and joins the fronts in shoulder and side seams. The single-breasted fronts are closed with buttons and buttonholes in a fly and above the closing they are reversed in lapels that form notches with the ends of the rolling collar. The sleeves are of comfortable width and pocket laps cover openings to side, left breast and change pockets. Machine-stitching gives a neat finish to all the edges of the coat.

The overcoat may be stylishly made up in broadcloth, melton, kersey or any cloth of solid or mixed hue suitable for overcoats. Machine-stitching will give the most appropriate completion.

Pattern No. 9349, *The Delineator,* **October 1897.**

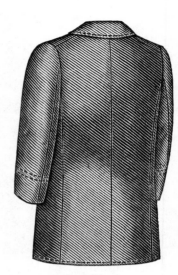

Front View.   *Back View.*

1897 Norfolk Suit

Illustration 176. The Norfolk suit pictured here is to be worn by five to twelve-year-old boys. It is made of fancy cheviot and finished with machine-stitching and buttons is fashionably known as the Tyrolean or chamois hunter's suit. The knickerbocker trousers are made with a fly and droop over the knees where they are drawn in with elastics. The Norfolk jacket consists of a yoke upper portion to which the back and fronts are sewn. A box plait is applied at the center of the back and similar plaits are arranged on the fronts at each side of the closing. Above the closing the front yokes are reversed in pointed lapels that meet the ends of the rolling coat collar in notches. Large patch pockets are stitched to the fronts back of the plaits; a belt passed beneath the plaits and under fanciful straps stitched over the side seams surrounds the waist. The comfortable sleeves are finished at the wrists with stitching and buttons.

The cap matches the suit. It consists of joined sections that meet in a point at the center under a button. The front of the cap droops over the visor.

Scotch tweed and heavy suitings will make up nicely in this suit for cold weather and flannel, serge and lightweight suitings may be selected for the intermediate seasons. Machine-stitching and buttons will provide a neat decorative finish. The cap will usually match the suit.

Pattern No. 9350, *The Delineator,* **October 1897.**

1897 Play Suit

Illustration 177. This style of play suit is most practical and is now almost invariably used by little men from three to sixteen years of age during play hours. Blue jean was used for the overalls or Brownie breeks as they are better known and gingham for the blouse. The blouse is plain and is drawn in about the waist by an elastic at the lower edge to droop in the customary way. The shirt sleeves are finished with straight cuffs; the sailor collar has pointed ends flaring at the throat. A spotted silk tie gives a neat finish.

The overalls or Brownie breeks reach to the waist at the back but in front they are extended in a bib that is upheld by straps starting at the upper edge of the back and buckled to the top of the bib. The legs reach well over the ankles and the overalls are closed at the sides. A patch pocket is stitched on each side of the front and two patch pockets are stitched on the right back.

Jean in blue or brown will always be used for the overalls but the blouse may be of flannel or serge.

The soft Tam O'Shanter cap is of navy blue English serge.

Pattern Nos. 8616 (blouse) and 1469 (overalls), *The Delineator*, **November 1897.**

Front View.

Back View.

1897 Pea Jacket

Illustration 178. Little boy's pea jacket or short overcoat.

Pattern No. 9414, *The Delineator*, **November 1897.**

Front View.

Back View.

1898 Suit

Illustration 179. This is a handsome suit for best wear, fashionably worn by little boys four to ten years of age. It is pictured made of velvet and trimmed with wide and narrow silk braid and gilt buttons. The back of the jacket is shaped by a center seam and is joined in shoulder and underarm seams to the fronts. These open all the way over a pretty vest, the lower front corners being rounded gracefully. Pocket laps trimmed with braid cover openings to inserted side pockets. A breast pocket in the left front is bound with braid. The two-seam sleeves are trimmed in cuff effect with braid and buttons. A rolling collar is at the neck.

The vest is fitted by shoulder and underarm seams and shaped to form two points below the closing, which is made at the center of the front with buttons and buttonholes. Openings to inserted pockets are bound with braid.

The short trousers are closed at the sides. They are shaped to fit closely by the usual seams and are finished with under-waistbands for attachment to an underwaist.

When intended for dressy wear the suit will be made of diagonal, camel's hair, English serge and so forth. Fancy mixed cheviots or tweeds will make serviceable everyday suits. A suit of dark red English serge may have a vest of black cloth and black soutache braid may supply the trimming.

Pattern No. 9703, *The Delineator,* **March 1898.**

Front View.

Back View.

1898 Blouse

Illustration 180. This comfortable and practical blouse for boys three to twelve years of age is pictured made of blue flannel with white flannel for the shield. Pipings of white flannel, an embroidered emblem and machine-stitching give the decorative finish. The blouse is shaped by shoulder and underarm seams and closed at the center of the front with a fly. The shield is attached with buttons and buttonholes and is closed at the back; it is finished with a narrow neckband. The lower edge of the blouse is turned under for a hem in which an elastic is run to draw the edge in closely about the waist, the blouse drooping in the characteristic manner. A convenient breast pocket is attached to the left front. The large sailor collar falls deep and square at the back and its pointed ends meet at the top of the closing. A box plait is formed in the sleeve from the top to the wrist on the upper side of the arm; the sleeves are gathered and completed with round cuffs that close with two buttons and buttonholes.

Such materials as camel's hair, serge and washable fabrics like gingham, piqué, lawn, linen and batiste will be chosen for the blouse and frequently a contrast will be arranged as suggested, with braid-pipings of the contrasting fabric and stitching for decoration. A blouse of this kind for wear with a plaid kilt skirt may be made of navy blue and red twilled flannel. The red flannel may be used for the shield and also for pipings to trim the sailor collar and cuffs.

Pattern No. 9688, *The Delineator,* **March 1898.**

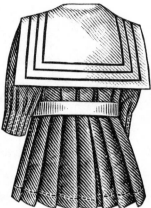

Front View.

Back View.

1898 Costume

Illustration 182. White and red flannel are united in this costume which produces a pleasing effect that is heightened by a decoration of red braid, an embroidered anchor and machine-stitching. The skirt is laid in backward-turning plaits back of a broad applied box plait under which the skirt is closed at the front; it is joined to the body in which at the back three box plaits are formed. A box plait is also laid on each front and between the fronts, which separate with a flare toward the shoulders is shown a buttoned-in shield that is finished with a narrow neck band. The shield is framed by the tapering curved ends of a large sailor collar that is square at the back and spreads over the sleeves; these are gathered at the top and laid in box plaits at the wrist, the plaits being stitched to cuff depth. A belt closed with a button and buttonhole is worn, but it may give place to a leather belt. This costume is appropriate for two to five-year-old boys.

Combinations are almost invariably arranged in sailor dresses, the shield usually being of a bright color with blue, gray, brown or green for the remainder. Braid is a pretty decoration and embroidered insertion or edging may be used to trim dresses of piqué or linen crash for which the mode is also suitable.

Pattern No. 9687, *The Delineator,* **March 1898.**

1898 Dress

Illustration 181. This dress for boys two to five years of age is trim and bright looking made of fancy light brown cheviot and red cloth with a simple decoration of black braid and an embroidered emblem. One box plait is made in each front and three in the back; the fronts open with a flare toward the shoulders over a long shield that is finished with a neck band and buttoned in. The large sailor collar shows tapering ends meeting at the bottom of the shield. Box plaits stitched to cuff depth collect the fullness at the wrists of the stylish sleeves. The skirt has a broad box plait applied on the front and is laid in backward-turning plaits at the sides and back; it is closed under the box plait and joined to the body. A belt with pointed ends closed with a button and buttonhole at the front adds to the jaunty effect. This dress is shown again in *Illustration 182.*

The dress would be effective developed in combinations of all woolen fabrics of suitable weight and also for summer wear in crash, linen or piqué. Braid is a satisfactory trimming on all materials.

The hat is of red cloth.

Pattern No. 9687, *The Delineator,* **March 1898.**

1898 Suit

Illustration 183. This suit is exceptionally jaunty for boys from two to five years of age. It is very effective as shown with the skirt made of plaid serge, the blouse of white lawn with the frills of lace edging and a decoration of lace insertion. The jacket is of black velvet. The skirt is laid in box plaits and attached to a sleeveless underwaist. The blouse has its lower edge drawn in about the waist by a tape in the hem and droops all round over the skirt. A frill of lace conceals the closing. The frill-bordered tab collar and roll-up cuffs are worn outside the short bolero jacket which has prettily rounded lower corners and comfortable coat sleeves.

The costume offers opportunity for many combinations. Woold goods, velvet and India silk could be united, with lace for trimming the silk blouse, or a piqué jacket, a lawn blouse trimmed with swiss or nainsook embroidered edging and a skirt of plaid or striped gingham or colored piqué could be associated.

The tam cap is of cloth.

Pattern No. 9704, *The Delineator,* **March 1898.**

1898 Costume

Illustration 184. This jacket is shown made of velvet, the blouse of fine lawn with the frills of embroidered edging and the skirt of piqué. It is shown differently in *Illustration 183*.

Pattern No. 9704, *The Delineator,* **March 1898.**

Front View.   *Back View.*

1898 Suit

Illustration 185. Dark blue flannel and white duck are united in this handsome suit which is fashionably known as the "cruiser suit," suitable for boys two to five years old. The pleasing effect is enhanced by a decoration of braid, buttons, an embroidered emblem and machine-stitching. The single-breasted vest of white duck is closed with buttons and buttonholes and the back is held in by the regulation straps. It is finished with a deep square sailor collar between the ends of which is seen a buttoned-in shield completed with a narrow neck band and decorated with an embroidered emblem. The sailor collar is worn outside the jacket, the fronts of which are reversed in shawl lapels by a moderately deep rolling collar and connected below the lapels by a strap buttoned on underneath. Inserted side pockets are finished with welts and the sleeves are well shaped. The back is made without a center seam. The short trousers are close fitting and are closed with a fly.

Serge, tweed, cheviot and duck are appropriate for the suit and crash may also be used. White and red cloth would form a dressy combination on which black or white braid would be effective decoration.

The tam cap is of white duck with a word-decorated band of ribbon.

Pattern No. 9673, *The Delineator,* **March 1898.**

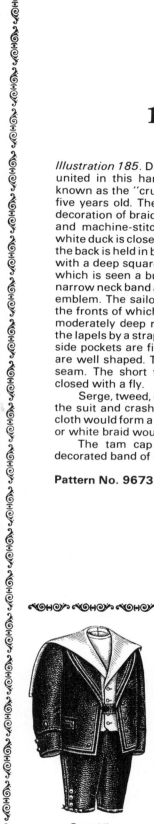

Front View.

Back View.

1898 Cruiser Suit

Illustration 186. This cruiser suit is shown differently developed in *Illustration 185*. In this instance it is made of velvet and white duck with wide and narrow braid, satin ribbon and buttons for decoration.

Pattern No. 9673, *The Delineator,* **March 1898.**

1899 Street Suit

Illustration 187. Winter street suit for young men.

The Delineator, **January 1899**.

NEW DESIGNS
FOR LITTLE MEN.

9532

9052

9960

9962

2212

2745

2571

1768

2589

9687

2213

7810

9054

9902

2707

9703

2089

9673

9346

9415

1899 Costumes

Illustrations 188 to 207. Styles for little men. Numbers below costumes denote pattern numbers.

June 1899 periodical.

NEW DESIGNS
FOR LITTLE MEN.

2010

2438

2682

9177

2746

2473

1694

8614

2586

9771

9056

2681

2541

2051

9020

2264

2791

9350

2792

8922

1899 Costumes

Illustrations 208 to 227. Styles for little men. Numbers below costumes denote pattern numbers.

June 1899 periodical.

90

1900 Costume

Illustration 228. The overcoat of this outfit is made of light box cloth, has a velvet collar and is corded with velvet down the front. The trousers are made of cheviot. The overcoat is fitted by center-back, side-back and shoulder seams. The side-back seams are left open about 4in (10.2cm) at the lower portion. A rolling collar finishes the neck edge and pocket flaps are attached to the fronts. The sleeve is two seamed and smoothly inserted in the armhole. The left side of the coat overlaps the right and fastens with buttons and buttonholes.

Kersey, melton, chinchilla, beaver or cheviot may be used to develop this pattern. Velvet cording or silk braid may be used to trim.

The trousers are shaped by center-back, inside and outside leg seams. They are fitted in the back by two darts and pocket openings occur about 1in (2.5cm) from the belt in the outside leg seams. The trousers close down the front center by means of a fly attachment and buttons and buttonholes.

This costume can be worn by boys five to twelve years of age.

Tweed, flannel, cheviot, plain cloth, whipcord, diagonal, velveteen, corduroy or serge may be used to develop the trousers. Braid or buttons may be effectively used to trim.

Pattern Nos. 5463 (coat) and 3588 (knee trousers), *The Designer,* **January 1900.**

1900 Russian Suit

Illustration 229. This Russian suit is made of brown cheviot and is trimmed with wide brown wool braid and small gilt buttons. It sets as loosely in the back as in the front. The suit consists of knickerbockers and blouse. The former garment has a lining to which the outer portion of the legs is caught at the knee, producing the baggy effect that is the feature of knickerbockers.

Pattern No. 5834, *The Designer,* **October 1900.**

1900 Suit

Illustration 230. For boys from eight to sixteen years of age a combination suit is stylish and serviceable. This one consists of a one-button cutaway sack coat and knee trousers with a fly. Both are made in the present instance of dark blue serge. With the coat it is necessary that a shirt, shirtwaist or blouse be worn.

Pattern No. 5628, *The Designer,* **October 1900.**

1900 Sailor Suit

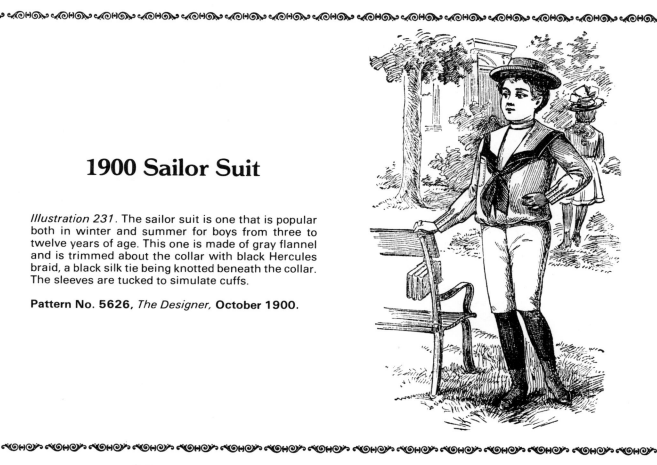

Illustration 231. The sailor suit is one that is popular both in winter and summer for boys from three to twelve years of age. This one is made of gray flannel and is trimmed about the collar with black Hercules braid, a black silk tie being knotted beneath the collar. The sleeves are tucked to simulate cuffs.

Pattern No. 5626, *The Designer,* **October 1900.**

1900 Suit

Illustration 232. A decidedly manly suit is this one with a trim cutaway coat, a vest which may be made single or double-breasted and knee trousers. The pictured suit is made of black cheviot and the double-breasted vest is used in this instance. This attractive outfit is made in sizes for boys three to eight years of age.

Pattern No. 5842, *The Designer,* **October 1900.**

1900 Suit

Illustration 233. For older boys, especially those who are going to school, the combination suit illustrated here is very stylish. It is composed of a Norfolk jacket and knickerbocker or Russian trousers. Both garments are cut in sizes for boys from three to twelve years of age and as pictured here are made of rough brown tweed. With the Norfolk may be worn a shirtwaist of any preferred design. The back of the Norfolk is arranged in pleats to match the front, and the belt may be slipped under them and closed with a buckle, or it mey be buttoned down as in this illustration. The trousers are baggy at the knees and may be buttoned to the shirtwaist or for larger boys may be supported by suspenders.

Pattern No. 5686, *The Designer,* **October 1900.**

1900 Kilt Suit

Illustration 234. Kilt suits are quite as fashionable for little boys as the Russian suits and by some mothers are even better liked. This kilt suit consists of an underwaist, skirt and jacket. The underwaist is faced to form a vest. As shown the suit is made of brown cashmere and the collar trimmed with gold braid and small gilt buttons. It is suitable for boys ranging from two to five years of age.

Pattern No. 5880, *The Designer,* **October 1900.**

1900 Kilt Suit

Illustration 235. Another kilt suit, this one being made of gray cloth with a collar of dark red cloth trimmed with rows of gray and scarlet silk braid. The shield is also made of the red cloth trimmed with the braid. This is a very pretty suit indeed and like the one previously described, it is appropriate for boys from two to five years of age.

Pattern No. 5836, *The Designer,* **October 1900.**

1900 Costume

Illustration 236. Much on the style of the Russian suit is this garment which has a diagonal closing and is arranged in two box pleats in the back. As pictured, it is made of smooth-faced green flannel and is trimmed in military style with black braid and black cloth-covered buttons. The collar is faced with black velvet and the belt, made of the same material, is held by a silver buckle.

Pattern No. 5998, *The Designer,* **October 1900.**

1900 Russian Costume

Illustration 237. For very little boys this Russian blouse is very becoming and suitable. In its pictured development it is made of dark red serge and is trimmed with bands of white cloth edged with black braid. The belt is held by a silver buckle and three small buttons trim the closing piece.

Pattern No. 5957, *The Designer,* **October 1900.**

1900 Russian Suit

Illustration 238. Another Russian suit, this one is to be worn by boys from three to twelve years of age. It is made as illustrated of blue cheviot serge with a collar and belt of white cloth, the former being trimmed with dark blue braid and the latter held by a steel buckle. The blouse sets rather loosely in the back and the collar falls over the shoulders in a large square. The lower part of the sleeves is tucked and stitched to form cuffs. The blouse is worn with knickerbockers.

Pattern No. 5627, *The Designer,* **October 1900.**

1900 Suits

Illustrations 239 to *242.* Variations of suits worn by boys in the fall of 1900.

The Designer, **October 1900.**

With any of the separate coats or waists mentioned, instead of knickerbockers or other knee trousers, long trousers may be worn. As a rule, schoolboys do not wear long trousers until their fourteenth year, and not then if they are undersized.

Winter hats for tiny boys will be broad-brimmed felts of Napoleonic, Rough Rider or Quaker shape, with brims bound with wide ribbon and simple trimming consisting of a folded silk band and a short quill or ribbon cockade. These hats, when possible, should match the suit or overcoat in color and the leggings will be worn by even little tots of one and two years.

Boys from six to twelve wear cadet caps in either army or navy style or soft crown roll-brim sailors of felt with merely a ribbon band. Lads from twelve to sixteen wear fedoras, wide-a-wakes or derbies, the fedora in gray being especially popular. An excellent school hat

that will stand all kinds of rough treatment and which can be manufactured at home is the polo cap made of the same material as the suit or the overcoat.

Boys from two to twelve wear spring-heeled shoes of box calf, either laced or button, the latter being preferable for the very little fellows. For more dressy wear fine calf with patent leather foxings are used; these nearly always button. Dark tan shoes are worn as much in the winter now as in the summer, but are scarcely serviceable for school wear as are those made of black calf.

In hosiery for boys, styles have not changed materially since last year. Ribbed wool stockings are worn on all occasions save for evening or dancing school, when fine lisle thread or silk take their place. No matter what the color of the suit, black stockings are worn with it, except by very little boys who wear white flannel or piqué suits in the winter afternoons and with these, white wool stockings are worn.

Little lads still in kilts wear wide silk or madras cravats tied in a large bowknot beneath the chin. These cravats are also worn by schoolboys from six to ten with shirtwaists or blouses. After the latter age the English square, four-in-hand or small flat bow ties are in style.

With regard to collars the high-band turn-down, or as the haberdashers call them, stand up turn-downs, are the newest for boys from six to sixteen. They are a comfortable as well as a stylish pattern and give the little fellows a manly look. The Eton collar with either square or rounded corners is also much worn, but the wide, deep sailor collar, which encircled the neck closely, then fell far down on the shoulders, is no longer in fashion for school or the street, though made of handsome embroidery or lace it is still worn with a velvet or fine cloth suit for the house or on dressy occasions.

Boys' trousers, to be stylish, should reach just over the bend of the knee. Knickerbockers are a trifle longer and may be fastened above or below the knee. Kilt skirts should be about the same length as the trousers. Beneath the kilt skirt should be worn short trousers made of cloth to match the kilt or of dark flannel. These are much neater and are far warmer for winter than the cotton drawers and petticoat, even for very little fellows. If a petticoat is preferred, it should be made of the same material or at least of the same color as the kilt, and it is scarcely necessary to say that it should be finished with a wide hem and nothing else in the way of trimming.

Among the materials which are in style for boys' general wear suits are serge, tweed, cheviot, unfinished wool, frieze and flannel. These may be used for Russian and kilt suits as well as for trousers suits. Russian suits for little fellows may also be made of ladies' cloth or broadcloth or even of cashmere. Suits for dancing school or more dressy wear are made of broadcloth, velvet or velveteen. Even very little boys wear vests, either single or double-breasted, with these more fanciful suits, and for the vests are used light tan, gray or white doeskin, white ribbed silk or novelty vesting, small pearl, silver or gilt buttons decorating and fastening the fronts. Sometimes the vests are made with lapel or shawl collars; sometimes they are plain. With these finer suits for dancing school or party are worn patent leather pumps or low shoes, or fine calfskin shoes with patent leather tips.

Tan, dark red or brown dogskin gloves heavily stitched and fastened with a single clasp are worn by boys of all ages, including the tots of two and three who wear Russian or kilt street suits. Dogskin mittens or fleece-lined gloves are used for school and general wear, and for dancing school and parties pearl-colored gloves of thinner kid with black stitching.

Among the minor details it may be mentioned that boys who are old enough to wear shirts with cuffs wear link buttons in preference to studs and the fronts of the shirts are fastened with small pearl buttons and buttonholes instead of studs and eyelets. Only the older lads wear made ties and scarf pins and even for them, the pin should be small and unobtrusive. Boys, in fact, are dressed in a much more manly fashion than in past years; curls and furbelows are considered out of place on them as soon as they are old enough to walk alone.

A few years ago it was the fashion for boys large and small to wear their hair in a bang over the forehead but this style is no longer in vogue. Little lads should have the hair cut in Russian style, that is to say, just long enough to rest on the edge of the collar in the back and at the sides, and in a deep, smooth bang in front. This cut completely hides the ears and while fashionable at present, is hardly becoming, although it goes well with the Russian blouse suits. The Russian cut is considered appropriate only for boys from two to seven years of age; older ones should have the hair at the sides and back cropped quite closely; in front it should be parted a little to either the right or left of the center.

Boys are put into trousers at a much earlier age nowadays than they were a few years ago. It is not an unusual thing to see mites of three and four clad in the most manly fashion, and it is undeniable that the little fellows seem more at their ease than when they were arrayed in frocks, flapping hats and so forth, in poor imitation of their sisters. It is all very well to make little court gentlemen of our embryo men with purple and fine linen, silken hose and dainty shoes on high days, but a genuine boy, to be healthy and happy — as all youngsters should be — must not be hampered by his garments, which accordingly must be made not too elaborately and of substantial material.

The Designer, **October 1900.**

1900 Suit

Illustration 243. As pictured, this suit is made of gray cloth trimmed with black braid and the blouse of white lawn, trimmed with embroidery. In the small view the jacket and collar corners are rounded and the suit is plainly developed. It is designed to be worn by boys three to seven years of age.

The back closing underwaist is fitted by underarm and shoulder seams and to it are buttoned the trousers which are made without a fly and have side openings. They are fitted by center seams, also inside leg seams. The blouse has shoulder and underarm seams. A casing and drawing strings adjust the fullness at the waistline; the neck edge is completed by a sailor collar. The one-seamed sleeve is finished at the wrist by a band and a turned-up cuff. The blouse closes down the

front and the short jacket is fitted by underarm and shoulder seams. The sleeves are two seamed.

Pattern No. 6198, *The Designer,* **December 1900.**

1902 Boys' Costumes

Illustrations 244 to *247.* Original designs by Mrs. Ralston.

Ladies' Home Journal, **March 1902.**

A DUCK REEFER

FOR A TINY BOY

A MILITARY BLOUSE

A LINEN SUIT

1902 Suit

Illustration 248. This stylish suit for boys from three to eight years old is made of dark gray serge and is trimmed with bands of white braid. The shield is of white piqué. The blouse is fitted by underarm and shoulder seams and the pattern provides yoke facings which may be used. The upper portions of the fronts are cut away in a V and a sailor collar is attached. When the yoke facing is not used, a pocket may be attached to the left breast of the blouse. The sleeve is a one-seamed model finished with a deep straight cuff which is closed at the outside of the arm by means of buttons and buttonholes or studs. Straps are attached to the underarm seams of the blouse and the belt is slipped through these. The fitted underwaist is faced to form a shield. A narrow band finishes the neck edge; the underwaist closes down the center of the back. The fullness at the waistline is shirred front and back and held by a belt. The trousers consist of a lining and outside portions, both fitted by inside leg seams and center seams, the fullness at the upper portion of the back being disposed in slanting darts. The fullness of the material at the lower edge of each trouser leg is disposed in gathers and turned up and attached to the lining.

Pattern No. 7186, *The Designer,* **April 1902.**

1902 Costume

Illustration 250. Boy's costume.

The Delineator, **July 1902.**

1902 Suit

*Illustration 249.*This stylish little suit appropriate for two to five-year-old boys is made of white piqué and is trimmed with embroidered piqué insertion. The long waist of the dress is fitted by underarm and shoulder seams; the fronts are cut away, thus forming a long, V-shaped opening which shows the vest piece. The latter is in one piece, finished at the upper edge by a band. A sailor collar is attached to the neck edge of the back of the waist and to the forward edges of the fronts. The box-plaited skirt is attached to the lower edge of the body portions, a belt concealing the joining. Small strap pieces are attached at the underarm seams at the waistline and the belt is slipped through them. The sleeve is one seamed, and the fullness at the wrist is disposed in scant stitched box plaits. If desired, however, a turn-up cuff may be attached.

Pattern No. 7212, *The Designer,* **April 1902.**

"OVER THE SEA WITH THE SAILOR"

1905 Costumes

Illustrations 251 to *254*. The date when the first sailor costume came in vogue is one of the forgotten facts in history, but it was long before any reader of this article can remember and from its first appearance, it was made welcome and has survived. It has undergone many variations to the present day, when, if possible, it is more fashionable than ever. Next to the "Buster Brown" dress, it is the most comfortable garb that a boy or girl, or even Madame herself, can assume, and the style lends itself to particularly effective development in summer fabrics.

For instance, what could be prettier or jauntier than the little suits and frocks shown in these illustrations? Boys and girls alike look happy and attractive in them. The first dress, a box-plaited model, is made of white linen and is trimmed with red washable braid. A scarlet silk tie and scarlet stockings and low shoes are worn with the little dress; completing the costume is a wide sailor hat of white straw with a scarlet band and bow. A shield fills in the neck of the blouse and this model is suitable for girls from four to thirteen years.

The suit next pictured is a combination of brown flannel and ecru linen, the linen portion being trimmed with brown braid. The sailor hat is of ecru straw and has a band of brown ribbon. Brown shoes and stockings complete the outfit which may be worn by boys from three to ten years. Another style of large collar is supplied with the suit, or the blouse may be made without the sailor collar and an Eton or other linen collar worn with it.

The dress on the third figure is of dark blue and white French percale, the sailor collar being of dark blue linen trimmed with bands of white linen and the shield of white linen. The hat is a white sailor with a blue band, the stockings dark blue and the shoes white kid with patent leather foxings. The dress is suitable for girls from four to fourteen years.

The last child in the group wears a tar suit of blue duck with a sailor collar and shield of white linen, the collar being widely bound with dark blue linen and trimmed with blue braid. The tar cap is of white duck with a glazed leather headband. The shoes are white kid and enamel leather foxing similar to those worn by the little girl next to him. The suit may be worn by boys from four to ten years of age.

The Designer, **April 1905.**

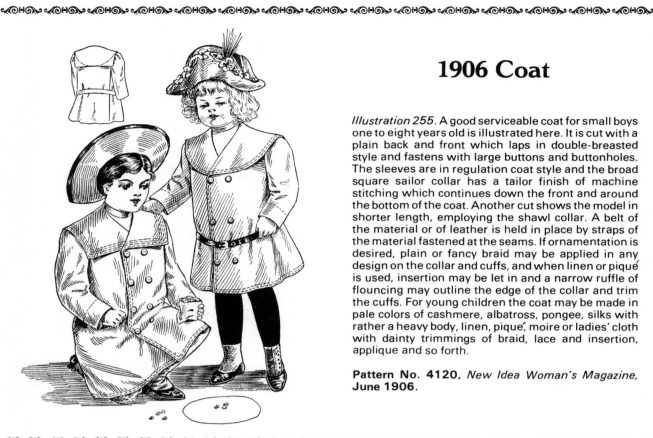

1906 Coat

Illustration 255. A good serviceable coat for small boys one to eight years old is illustrated here. It is cut with a plain back and front which laps in double-breasted style and fastens with large buttons and buttonholes. The sleeves are in regulation coat style and the broad square sailor collar has a tailor finish of machine stitching which continues down the front and around the bottom of the coat. Another cut shows the model in shorter length, employing the shawl collar. A belt of the material or of leather is held in place by straps of the material fastened at the seams. If ornamentation is desired, plain or fancy braid may be applied in any design on the collar and cuffs, and when linen or piqué is used, insertion may be let in and a narrow ruffle of flouncing may outline the edge of the collar and trim the cuffs. For young children the coat may be made in pale colors of cashmere, albatross, pongee, silks with rather a heavy body, linen, piqué, moire or ladies' cloth with dainty trimmings of braid, lace and insertion, applique and so forth.

Pattern No. 4120, *New Idea Woman's Magazine,* **June 1906.**

1906 Apron

Illustration 256. Blue chambray with a white piqué collar, pastron and cuffs were used in making this boy's Russian blouse and with it is worn a belt of black patent leather. It is designed to be worn by two to eight year olds. The blouse portion buttons at the front; a sailor collar finishes the neck. The sleeves, which are in full length, are completed by a turned-back cuff; a shield with standing collar and embroidered emblem fastens at the back. An elastic or tape regulates the fullness of the knickerbockers at the knee, though the lower edge may be gathered and finished with a band instead. Loops of the material sewn at the side seams hold the belt in place; this may be of the material or of leather. For summer wear suits of this kind are more serviceable if made of wash material as they will require many trips to the laundry. For morning wear, blue, gray, tan or plaids will be satisfactory with the shield of white linen. To wear for afternoon, white is given first choice and linen, piqué, serge and flannel are suggested. The garment is also suitable for a girl and petticoats may be worn underneath instead. This suit can be worn by children of ages two to eight.

Pattern No. 4150, *New Idea Woman's Magazine,* **July 1906.**

1906 Costume

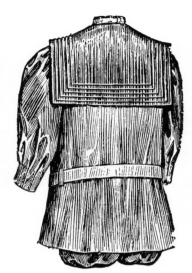

Illustration 257. The fitted blouse of this suit (for two to six-year-old boys) is confined at the waistline by a belt. A sailor or small shawl collar may be used and the one-seamed sleeve is plaited to cuff depth. A pocket is inserted in the left front of the blouse and a removable shield is supplied. The knickerbockers are fitted by inside and outside leg seams also center back and front seams. The lower edges are finished with casings and elastics.

Pattern No. 2120, *The Designer,* **December 1906.**

1906 Rompers

Illustration 258. These serviceable rompers are made of blue jean and are fitted by underarm and shoulder seams, the lower edges being gathered into buttoned bands. A turn-down collar or circular neck band may finish the high or round neck. A patch pocket is supplied and the one-seamed sleeve may be made in full or elbow length.

Pattern No. 2100, *The Designer,* **December 1906.**

PRACTICAL LESSONS IN GARMENT-MAKING.—No. 15.

ORNAMENTAL TACKS AND EMBROIDERED ORNAMENTS.

The simplest staying tack, known as the bar-tack, is shown partly made at figure No. 1. It is much used at the ends of pocket openings, etc. The detail of this tack is as follows: First decide on the length of the tack, marking the line with chalk; then pass the needle up from underneath at one end of the line, down through at the opposite end, up again at the starting point, and down again at the opposite end; and make as many of these long stitches as desired. Not less than two stitches should be made, but as many more may be made as the worker may elect—the greater the number, the thicker and heavier will be the tack. Then, without breaking the thread, bring the needle up at one end, just to one side of the upper and under long stitches, and pass it down at a point exactly opposite on the other side of the long stitches, to form a short stitch that will be square across the long stitches on top. Cover the entire length of the long stitches with such short stitches, being careful to bring the needle up at the same side of the long stitches every time, so that the *under* part of the long stitches will be crossed as well as the *upper* part, and pressing the long stitches together with the needle so as to produce as narrow and high an effect as possible.

In garments that are finished with machine-stitching, bar-tacks at the ends of pocket openings usually extend from a second row of stitching above the opening to a second row below the opening, and are sometimes crossed at the ends with short bar-tacks, as illustrated at figure No. 2.

Tacks that are commonly called arrow-heads are seen in a variety of shapes and stitches, and are made at the tops of plaits and laps and at the ends of seams and pocket openings. One of the simplest of these tacks is illustrated in detail at figure No. 3, and completed at figure No. 4. To make this style of tack, mark an outline of the tack with chalk or a pencil. Bring the needle up through at point A and pass it down at point B; then up inside and very close to point B, and down on the center line close to point A; up at point A, exactly where the needle was first passed through and down at point C; up inside and close to point C, and down on the center line exactly at the second stitch extending from B to A. Fill in the entire outline in this way, always making two stitches on one side and then two on the other, and being careful to keep all the stitches even on the center line. At figure No. 3 the work is shown with three stitches on one side and two on the other, and the needle correctly placed for the fourth stitch on line BA.

A more artistic and durable arrow-head is depicted completed at figure No. 10, and in detail at figures Nos. 5, 6, 7, 8 and 9. Mark the outline with chalk or a pencil. Bring the needle up at point A, and pass it down at point B; then up inside and very close to point B, down on the line AC close to point A, and up at point A outside and very close to the first stitch made. Then pass the needle under the second stitch and down at point C, as illustrated at figure No. 5. Bring the needle up inside and close to point C and then pass it down near point A outside and very close to the first stitch made, as shown at figure No. 6. Next bring the needle up outside and very close to the first stitch running from A to C, and quite close to the second stitch in line AB; and then pass it down near B, as illustrated at figure No. 7. Bring the needle up again on line BC inside and close to the third stitch in line AB; and pass it down outside the first stitch on line AC, as represented at figure No. 8. Then bring the needle up outside and very close to the first stitch on the line AB, pass it under the fourth stitch in line AB and down on line CB, close to the second stitch on line AC, as illustrated at figure No. 9. Now bring the needle up on line CB close to the third stitch on line AC, and pass it down outside the first stitch on line AB close to the third stitch on line AC. Proceed in this manner to fill in the outline, always making two stitches parallel with line AB, then two stitches parallel with line AC, and being careful to pass the third, fifth, seventh, etc., stitches, running parallel with line AC, respectively under the second, fourth, sixth, eighth, etc., stitches running parallel with line AB, as illustrated at figures Nos. 5 and 9.

Other fanciful arrow-heads are displayed at figures Nos. 11 and 12. They are worked exactly as described for that shown at figure No. 10.

The diamond ornament represented at figure No. 13 is made by working close together two arrow-heads like that shown at figure No. 12.

Every point of the star ornament portrayed at figure No. 15 is filled in exactly as described for working the arrow-head illustrated at figure No. 10. One point should be completely filled in at a time. The correct outline for a five-pointed star is given at figure No. 14, and the size displayed at this figure will prove effective for decorative purposes. The star may be copied on tracing-paper and the tracing used as a pattern; or, if a larger or smaller star be desired, a circle may be drawn, as indicated by the dotted line, and divided into five equal parts, and the points may then be carefully formed. One point in the outline is shown completely filled in, while another shows the detail of the work as described at figure No. 9.

Probably the most ornamental of the fancy tacks ordinarily used at the ends of pocket openings and seams is the crow-tack. It is illustrated completed at figure No. 18, and in detail at figures Nos. 16 and 17. Outline the tack with chalk or a pencil. The dotted outline seen at figure No. 16 shows the correct outline for the tack. Bring the needle up at point A, and pass it down at B, and up again at B outside and close to the stitch in line A B, then down at C, up at C outside and close to the stitch in line BC, and down at A just outside the stitch in line AB, as illustrated at figure No. 16. Now bring the needle up on dotted line AC outside the stitch on line AC close to A; and pass it down on dotted line BC outside the stitch on line BC close to B; up on dotted line AB outside both stitches on line AB close to B; down on dotted line CA outside the stitch on line CA close to C; up on dotted line BC outside both stitches on line BC; and down on dotted line AB outside both stitches on line AB, as illustrated at figure No. 17. Fill in the entire outline in this way, until the completed tack looks like figure No. 18. It will be noticed in making this tack that all the stitches are taken on the dotted lines and always outside the made stitches, thus compressing the stitches so as to curve the sides of the tack.

A basket pattern in square and diamond shapes is produced on the ornaments shown at figures Nos. 21 and 22. The diamond or square should be outlined in the size required with chalk or a pencil, and the sides should be marked off evenly into three, five, seven or more spaces, according to the size of the basket pattern desired—the

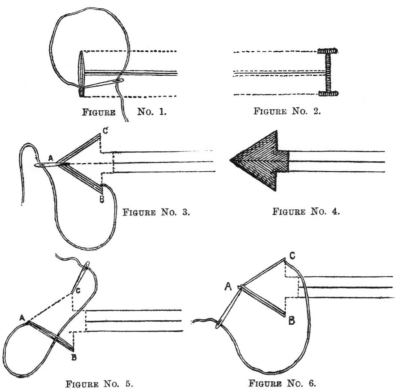

FIGURE No. 1.

FIGURE No. 2.

FIGURE No. 3.

FIGURE No. 4.

FIGURE No. 5.

FIGURE No. 6.

FIGURE No. 7.

FIGURE No. 8.

FIGURE No. 9.

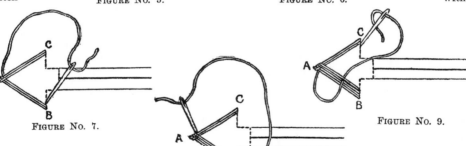

FIGURE No. 10.

FIGURE No. 11.

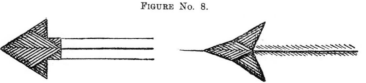

FIGURE No. 12.

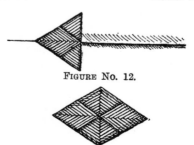

FIGURE No. 13.

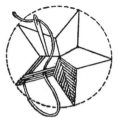

FIGURE NO. 14.

greater the number of spaces the smaller the basket pattern will be when worked.

The work is illustrated in detail at figures Nos. 19 and 20. Outline a square and mark off each side into three equal spaces. Bring the needle up at corner A, and pass it down at B, up close to B on line BC, and down close to A on line AD, as illustrated at figure No.

under and over the groups of stitches in the spaces.

The diamond ornament illustrated at figure No. 22 is worked exactly like the square, and so is every variety of ornament in even basket pattern.

The anchor is a very graceful ornament for sailor suits, etc.; and when correctly outlined, it requires very little labor to produce a good effect. It may be

FIGURE NO. 15.

19. Fill in the square in this way, being careful to make the same number of stitches in each marked-off space, and enough stitches to thoroughly cover the goods. In this instance twenty-seven stitches were used to fill in the square— nine in each space.

To make the basket pattern: Bring the needle up at corner C outside and close to the last stitch in line DC; pass it, eye first (so as not to split the thread), under the nine stitches in the middle space, as illustrated at figure No. 20; and then pass it down at corner

B outside and close to the first stitch on line AB. Now bring the needle up close to this stitch on line AB, and pass it under the same nine stitches in the same way, and down near the corner C. Continue in this way until nine stitches are made in this space. Now make nine stitches in the next space, passing the needle *under* the first group of nine, *over* the second group of nine and *under* the remaining group of nine. The last group of nine stitches is made exactly as directed for the first group.

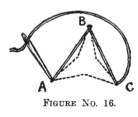

FIGURE NO. 16.

FIGURE NO. 17.

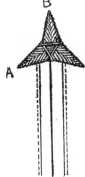

FIGURE NO. 18.

FIGURE NO. 19.

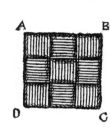

FIGURE NO. 20.

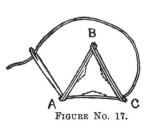

FIGURE NO. 21.

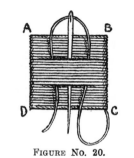

FIGURE NO. 22.

of any size, to suit the location for which it is intended. Three useful sizes are illustrated at figures Nos. 23, 24 and 25. Mark the outline with chalk or a pencil; then fill in the outline with long stitches, catching them to the material wherever necessary to keep them within the outline, and making a sufficient number of stitches to form a padding thick enough to produce a high rolled effect when the embroidery stitches are worked in. Work the points of the anchor exactly as directed for fancy arrow-heads, the detail of which is illustrated and described at figures Nos. 5, 6, 7, 8 and 9. Work in the embroidery stitches, passing the needle in at one side of the outline and out at the opposite side, making the stitches in over-and-over style and very close together, and being careful to take the stitches evenly on the outline and to draw them to an equal tension. The anchor may be outlined to slant to the right or to the left, as required, and may be traced on tracing paper, and the tracing cut out for a pattern that can be placed as desired.

FIGURE NO. 23.

FIGURE NO. 24.

FIGURE NO. 25.

Any number of spaces may be fitted in this way, the needle being passed alternately

These tacks and ornaments are generally worked with coarse button-hole twist.

GLOSSARY

ALBATROSS: a lightweight woolen fabric with a varied plain weave which produces a crepe effect.

APPLIQUE: a cutout decoration which is fastened to a larger piece of fabric.

ARMSEYE: the opening in a dress top or bodice for inserting a sleeve.

BALBRIGGAN: a jersey-type knot of cotton or wool used for underwear.

BATISTE: a soft, fine, sheer fabric with a plain weave.

BEDFORD CORD: a fabric with lengthwise ribs which resembles corduroy.

BENGALINE: a fabric with a crosswise rib.

BIAS: diagonally cut cloth used chiefly as a trim.

BOX CLOTH: a coarse, thick melton cloth, frequently in a buff color.

BRAID: ribbon or cord which usually has three or more component strands.

BREECHING: The change made in a small boy's clothing when he graduated from kilts (skirts) to pants, usually sometime between four and six years of age.

BROADCLOTH: a twilled, napped, worsted or woolen fabric with a dense texture and a smooth lustrous face.

BROWNIE BREEKS: a type of overalls or play trousers.

CAMBRIC: a thin, fine white linen cloth or a cotton fabric which resembles true cambric.

CAMEL'S HAIR CLOTH: a lightweight but warm coating fabric usually in a twill weave with a high gloss. Camel's hair cloth is made entirely or partially of camel's hair or mohair. A shade of tan is prevalent.

CANVAS: a firm, closely woven cloth made usually of hemp, linen or cotton.

CASHMERE (CASSIMERE): a soft twilled fabric made originally from fine cashmere wool from the undercoat of the Kashmir goat.

CASING: the space formed between two parallel lines of stitching through two or more layers of cloth into which something such as a string or elastic may be inserted.

CHAMBRAY: a lightweight fabric with colored warp and white filling yarns.

CHAMOIS: a soft pliant leather prepared from the skin of the chamois (small goatlike antelope) or from sheepskin.

CHEVIOT: a rough, heavy napped twill or plain fabric of coarse worsted or wool.

CHINA SILK: a transparent lustrous fabric in a plain weave. It is light or medium lightweight of silk or part silk.

CHINCHILLA: a twilled heavy woolen coating.

COCKADE: a rosette or similar ornament worn as a badge on a hat.

CORDUROY: a durable, usually cotton pile fabric with vertical wales or ribs.

COVERT CLOTH: a medium weight durable fabric in a diagonal twill weave.

CRASH: a coarsely woven fabric having a rough texture attributed to knotted or uneven yarn.

CRAVAT: a scarf or band worn around the neck.

CUFF: a turned-back hem.

DART: a stitched tapering fold in clothing.

DERBY: a stiff felt hat with narrow brim and dome-shaped crown.

DIAGONAL: a woolen twilled fabric in heavy or medium weight.

DIMITY: a sheer fabric, corded or cross-barred, figured or plain.

DOUBLE-BREASTED: having one-half of the front lapped over the other with a double row of buttons and a single row of buttonholes.

DUCK: a closely woven cotton or linen fabric in a plain weave. It is of a heavy weight; however, it is finer and lighter than canvas.

ECRU: a color in the beige family.

FALL: a front closure for boys' pants consisting of a rectangle of varying width across the front and attached by buttons at or near the waistline. Under the rectangle is a band extending from the side seams to center front which buttons to hold the pants up, and which holds the buttons for the fall. The underpart is called a FALL-BEARER.

FEATHERSTITCHING: an embroidery stitch which consists of a line of diagonal blanket stitches which are worked alternately to the left and right.

FEDORA: a low soft felt hat which has a crown creased lengthwise.

FLANNEL: a soft-twilled worsted or wool fabric having a loose texture and slightly napped surface.

FRIEZE: an embroidered fabric.

FROG: an ornamental braiding used to fasten the front of a garment which consists of a button and a loop through which it passes.

GALATEA: a sturdy cotton fabric of fine quality in a satin weave. It is a printed, white or dyed colored cloth, also striped. This fabric was used chiefly for play clothes for children. Named for a Greek sea nymph.

GIMP: an ornamental round cord or flat braid used as a trim.

GINGHAM: a fabric usually of yarn-dyed cotton with a plain weave.

GRASS LINEN: a loosely woven cloth, very durable and made of tough grass or vegetable fibers.

HATS: *Turkish* hat — made like a fez with a long tassel. *Scotch* hat — copied from standard Scottish costume and worn by both girls and boys. *Brewer's* or *Fisherman's* hat — a knitted stocking hat with a tassel at the end. (See *Introduction* for other styles.)

HERCULES BRAID: a corded braid used as a trim.

HOMESPUN: a durable woolen fabric in a twill or plain weave.

HOPSACKING: a rough-surfaced linen, cotton or rayon fabric of a plain weave. It is usually coarse like original jute and hemp sacking.

INDIA SILK: a thick, plain-woven silk fabric.

IRISH-POINT EMBROIDERY: cut-work embroidery.

JABOT: a pleated frill of lace or cloth attached down the center front of a costume.

JERSEY: a plain knitted, very elastic ribbed fabric. It is usually made of wool or worsted but can also be rayon, cotton or silk.

KERSEY: a coarse ribbed woolen fabric.

KILT: a knee-length pleated skirt worn by boys from two to six years of age; also refers to girls' pleated skirts.

KNICKERBOCKER: (see knickers).

KNICKERS: loose-fitting short trousers which are gathered at the knee.

LAPEL: the fold on the front of a garment which is usually a continuation of the collar.

LAWN: a fine, sheer cotton or linen fabric of plain weave which is thinner than cambric.

LEGGING: a covering of leather or cloth for the leg.

LINEN: a fabric made of flax and noted for its strength, luster and coolness.

LINEN CRASH: a coarsely woven fabric made of linen.

LISLE: a smooth, tightly twisted thread frequently made of long staple cotton.

MADRAS: a finely woven fabric, usually of cotton. It frequently has a design, varied from plaid to white or a bright color.

MARSEILLES: a firm cotton cloth which is similar to pique.

MELTON: a smooth, heavy woolen cloth with a short nap.

MIDDY BLOUSE: a blouse made after the fashion of midshipmen with a wide collar at the back and a V-neck with braid or scarf.

MOHAIR: a cloth of yarn made wholly or in part of the silky long hair of the Angora goat.

MOIRE: the irregular wavy finish on a cloth or fabric.

NAINSOOK: a lightweight soft muslin.

OVERALLS: trousers of strong material, usually having shoulder straps and a bib.

PASSEMENTERIE: trimmings, especially heavy embroideries or edgings.

PATCH POCKET: a flat pocket applied to the outside of a garment.

PATENT LEATHER: leather with a smooth, glossy hard finish.

PEA JACKET: a double-breasted heavy woolen jacket.

PERCALE: a fine closely woven fabric.

PIPING: trimming stitched along edges of clothing or in seams.

PIQUE: a durable ribbed cloth of rayon, silk or cotton.

PLASTRON: a trimming like a bib or dickey.

POLKA DOT: a dot in a pattern of regularly distributed dots in a fabric.

POMPON: a tuft or ball used as an ornamental trim.

PONGEE: a soft thin tan or ecru fabric of Chinese origin and woven from raw silk.

REEFER: a close-fitting, usually double-breasted jacket of heavy fabric.

RUCHING: strips of crepe, silk, lace, chiffon or other fabric and usually pleated or gathered.

RUSSIAN SUIT OR BLOUSE: a rather long tunic or blouse with a front left-side closing leading to a mandarin or stand-up collar, worn with a sash and full sleeves.

SACKING: a coarse and loosely woven cotton fabric.

SAILOR SUIT: also referred to as a middy suit, a Jack Tar suit or a Man-of-War suit.

SASH: a band worn over the shoulder or about the waist.

SATIN: a fabric in satin weave with a dull back and lustrous face.

SEERSUCKER: a light fabric of cotton, linen or rayon, usually striped and slightly puckered.

SERGE: a durable twilled fabric with a smooth, clear face as well as a pronounced diagonal rib on the front and on the back.

SHIELD: similar to a plastron or dickey.

SHOT: a fabric of changeable color.

SILK: a fine fabric made from silk filaments.

SOUTACHE: a narrow braid having a herringbone pattern used as a trim.

STUD: a solid button having a shank or eye on the back which, when inserted through an eyelet in a garment, acts as a fastener or an ornament.

SURAH: a soft twilled fabric of rayon or silk.

TASSEL: a dangling ornament made by laying a bunch of thread or cords parallel and fastening them at one end.

TREFOIL: a symbol or ornament in the form of a stylized trifoliate leaf.

TWEED: a rough woolen fabric made often in twill weaves.

ULSTER: a loose and long heavy cord.

VELVET: a fabric of silk, rayon or wool characterized by a short soft dense pile.

VIENNA: a soft fabric made from the wool of the vicuna.

WELT: a doubled edge insert, seam or strip for ornament or reinforcement.

WHIPCORD: a fabric which is made of hard-twisted yarns and having fine diagonal cords or ribs.

WORSTED: a fabric made from worsted yarns which tend to be smooth and strong.

YOKE: a shaped or fitted piece at the shoulder of various garments or at the top of a shirt.

ZOUAVE: a full skirt or jacket which resembles trousers worn by the French Zouaves.

PATTERN FOR BOY'S KILT
SIZE 17in (43.2cm) DOLL

Pattern 1

These boys' suits were adapted from *The Delineator* by Hazel Ulseth and Helen Shannon for (*Boys' Fashions 1885 to 1905*). The 17in (43.2cm) pattern No. 2340, November 1888, was designed for boys two to six years of age. The suit is presented in brown silk with contrasting beige vest and trim. A pleated kilt is attached to a waist to which is sewn a beige vest with pocket laps and a standing collar. Small buttons trim the vest, the jacket front, accentuate the box pleat and add a decorative touch to the back laps.

The 19in (48.3cm) pattern No. 9248, September 1885, was designed for boys from six to twelve years old. A sailor suit with long-flared pants topped by a jaunty sailor hat is made up in navy blue cotton with a blue and white-striped dickey and red braid trim.

GENERAL INSTRUCTIONS

1. PLEASE read through the whole pattern before starting to work.
2. Cut all pattern pieces other than trim of lightweight unbleached muslin or cotton. Assemble following instructions for suit, using longest stitch on machine. Fit as you go along to assure that this pattern fits your doll. (For very precise fitting instructions, see *Antique Doll Fashions* by Ulseth and Shannon.) Mark corrections with pencil or pen and transfer to tissue paper pattern. (If corrections are done carefully and do not involve major changes or use of additional material, basic unbleached muslin can be altered and used as lining for suit.
3. Seam allowances are 1/4in (.65cm) unless otherwise noted.

SPECIAL NOTE:

Kilts were normally attached to a waist with buttons all around. We have simplified this by machine-stitching the skirt to the waist.

FABRIC SUGGESTIONS

FOR WINTER: Thin soft velvet, suiting, cotton plaid, cotton twill, fine wool, cheviot, tricot, flannel, serge or tweed.

FOR SUMMER:

Piqué, gingham, silk, surah, percale or seersucker.

FABRIC REQUIREMENTS

17in (43.2cm) Doll

Lining: Small pieces of muslin.

Suiting, dark color: 24in (61cm) by 45in (114.3cm).

Suiting, light color: 12in (30.5cm) square.

Leather for hat: Two leather gloves about 3in (7.6cm) above wrist in length.

Buttons: 33 buttons about 1/4in (.65cm) in diameter.

CUTTING INSTRUCTIONS

UNDERWEAR: Using a knit fabric such as an old T-shirt.

CI. SHIRT: Cut 2 fronts and 1 back.

PANTS: Cut 2 of pattern and mark dart lightly.

JACKET, VEST, KILT and LINING:

C2. KILT WAIST: Lining for waist cut of unbleached muslin 4 fronts and 2 backs (it will be double thickness).

SKIRT LINING: Cut 1 rectangle 4 3/4in (12.2cm) by 42in (106.6cm).

JACKET LINING: Cut 2 centerbacks, 2 sidebacks, 2 fronts for innerlinings, 2 upper sleeves and 2 under sleeves. Fronts will be innerlined with muslin and lined with vest fabric. (If suit fabric is heavy, the innerlining may be omitted).

CAP: See cap pattern.

SUITING FABRIC, DARK COLOR

C3. SKIRT: Cut 1 rectangle 7½in (19.1cm) by 42in (106.6cm).

JACKET: Cut 2 centerbacks, 2 sidebacks, 2 fronts, 1 neck facing, 2 back facings for jacket hem 1½in (3.8cm) by 3in (7.6cm), 2 upper sleeves and 2 under sleeves.

SUITING FABRIC, LIGHT COLOR

C4. VEST: Cut 4 vest fronts, 1 collar, 2 pocket laps, 2 back laps and 4 cuffs.

ASSEMBLY INSTRUCTIONS

UNDERWEAR

SHIRT

A1. Using 1 back and 2 fronts, machine-stitch shoulder and side seams. Staystitch around neckline and armseyes.

A2. Centerfront: Use a scrap of cotton fabric about 5/8in (1.6cm) wide to reinforce front plackets, tacking in place before folding on foldline, to prevent stretching. Turn on foldline, turn edge 1/4in (.65cm) and hem by hand to form placket or centerfront opening. Close with buttons and hand-sewn buttonholes or snap fasteners.

A3. Shirt and Pants: To complete armseyes, neck edge bottom of shirt and pants legs, use any one of the following suggestions:
   (1) Turn edge once and machine-stitch.
   (2) Turn edge once and crochet with fine thread in a simple picot stitch.
   (3) Turn edge and blanket-stitch in place.
   (4) Bind edges with narrow bias tape.

PANTS

A4. Matching notches, machine-stitch centerfront and centerback seams, using flatfelled seams. Matching notches, machine-stitch crotch seams.

A5. Make casing at top, turning 1/8in (.31cm) and then on fold line, machine-stitch. Insert very narrow (1/8in [.65cm]) elastic.

A6. Try pants on doll and using dart lines as guide, hold in to fit legs. Sew darts and trim seams to 1/4in (.65cm). Complete pant legs, (see A3).

KILT WAIST

A7. Using 1 front section and 2 back sections, sew shoulder seams and press.

A8. Using second set of 1 front and 2 backs, sew shoulder seams and press.

A9. With right sides of the two assemblies together, match shoulder seams, side seams and centerbacks. Starting at waistline centerback, sew up both centerbacks to neckline; then sew around neckline. Clip to stitching around neckline, turn right sides out, one top fitting into the other, thus showing a finished neckline and centerbacks in one operation.

A10. Sew sideseams of 1 top set; then sew side seams of inside set, separately. Place on doll to check neckline for snug fit and for amount of overlap for plackets.

A11. Turn tiny hem around armseyes and handstitch.

Note: Armseyes may be sewn in same operation, before turning inside out, sew armseyes. Turn by working centerback sections through front, which will result in completely finished edges for armseyes, neckline and centerbacks.

A12. Turn 3/8in (.9cm) seam allowance at bottom of waist, handling inside and outside separately. Skirt will be enclosed between these two layers of cloth.

NECKLINE: Collar

A13. Turn seam allowances on both long edges of collar. Fold lengthwise, raw edges OUT, and handstitch ends. Turn right sides out and press. Tack edges together. Place around neckline of waist on doll, edges just touching, and pin in place. When it fits to your satisfaction, blindstitch lightly on right side; then re-stitch on wrong side more securely.

SKIRT

A14. Place skirt suiting rectangle on skirt lining, right sides together with bottom edges matching and machine-stitch. Turn and press. Bring top edges together (thus forming a 1½in (3.8cm) hem at bottom) and baste. Press at hem edge.

SKIRT PLEATING

A15. Place skirt on pleating pattern, *Illustration No. 1*, matching centerfront, and mark pleats on left end of skirt as shown, noting that Pleat No. 1 is part of the centerfront box pleat. Pin pleats in place and tailor-tack (or baste loosely). Press.

A16. Note *Illustration No. 2* showing treatment of LEFT END placket. Complete as shown. (Note: Right end laps over left end, the two end pleats coming together at overlap).

A17. Repeat this process for right end, reversing the pattern. On both sides of centerfront there will be 9 pleats. Note line on illustration which is a TACKLINE for the 9th pleat on the right end. Turn end to inside, work from wrong side to tack, thus completing 9th pleat.

A18. Join placket to within 3in (7.6cm) of top, forming placket opening (or do this after attaching skirt to waist top).

JOINING SKIRT to WAIST

A19. Place waist top edge over skirt top 3/8in (.9cm) matching ends and centerfront. Close pleats in slightly to fit waist and machine-stitch in place. On underside of garment tack waist lining in place.

COMPLETE KILT CLOSURE

A20. Complete kilt by sewing hooks and threaded loops at centerback to form closure.

VEST

A21. Matching 2 right sides to their corresponding self-fabric linings. machine-stitch in this order:
(a) armseyes, (b) shoulder seams, (c) across

bottom edge and clip where necessary. Turn right sides out and press, checking carefully to press exactly at seam line.

A22. Lay fronts together, lapping from left to right, and baste in place. Sew 7 buttons down centerfront as shown.

A23. Lay vest over waist front matching neckline, sideseams and armseyes. Tack in place. Note: Vest shoulder seams will extend ¼in (.65cm) beyond waist shoulder seam).
Turn under raw edge of side seam and tack in place. With neck edge of vest meeting collar, blindstitch in place around neckline.

POCKET FLAPS

A24. Fold lengthwise, stitch short ends, turn right sides out and press. Sew pocket flaps in place on line shown on pattern.

JACKET ASSEMBLY

A25. Lining jacket front: Place innerlinings on light-color fabric lining and baste. With right sides of jacket front and jacket linings touching, sew from O.......O, following arrows. Clip as shown, Turn right sides out and press, being careful to press exactly along seamline. Baste all around stitched area.

A26. Lining jacket back: Using unbleached muslin back linings and jacket backs, lay linings on corresponding jacket fabric and baste all around.

BACK LAP TRIM

A27. Using 2 laps of light fabric, fold lengthwise and sew short edges. Turn right sides out and press. Baste in place along sidebacks where shown on pattern.

BACK SEAMS

A28. Matching notches, pin and machine-stitch center-backs and side back seams. Note that centerback seam is open 2in (5.1cm) from bottom edge when completed. Press seams open and hem seam allowances of centerbacks for opening.

JOINING BACK and FRONTS

A29. Pin and machine-stitch jacket front and jacket back shoulder seams.

A30. Matching notches pin and machine-stitch side seams of jacket, BUT DO NOT STITCH LINING side seams at this point. Again, note special direction for stitching on pattern, which leaves ¼in (.65cm) overhang at bottom of jacket, and at neckline. Press seams open.

FACINGS

A31. Neck Facing: Place neck facing around back neckline, right sides together and handstitch carefully along seamline. Clip seam, turn, press and tack facing flat.

A32. Back hem facing: Place hem facing on back of jacket, right sides together, sew across bottom, press, turn to inside and tack facings in place.

SUIT TRIM

A33. Jacket front. Turn jacket upper revers and lower front revers as shown on pattern. Do not press, as they will be held in place by buttons. Hold in place by 3 buttons on each top rever, and 1 button on each lower rever.

A34. Jacket back: Sew 4 buttons on each back lap as shown.

SLEEVES

A35. Place linings on corresponding upper and under

sleeves, and baste all around. Matching notches of upper and lower sleeve, stitch by machine, press seams open.

A36. Setting sleeves: At top of sleeves, machine-stitch 2 rows of stitching, one on seam allowance and 1-⅛in (.31cm) from cut edge. Pull thread to "cup" sleeves. Matching notches, baste sleeves in place. Try on doll for fit, and also check sleeve length. Sew sleeves in by hand and turn bottom edge at correct length and hem.

CUFF
A37. Machine-stitch along 2 long sides and one short side. Turn right sides out and press. Pin to finished sleeve ⅛in (.31cm) from bottom of sleeve, the finished edge of cuff lying along the back seam. Blindstitch cuff edges in place and add 2 buttons on each cuff for trim.

BOY'S CAP (for 17in (43.2cm) Doll)
Note: A pair of brown leather gloves is suggested, whose tops extend at least 2in (5.1cm) above wrist. If piecing is necessary, piece the crown in two segments, or even four. Instructions given here are for LEATHER.

If fabric is used it will be necessary to add seam allowances where none are indicated for leather.

CUTTING INSTRUCTIONS
CI. LEATHER: Cut 1 crown, 1 brim, 2 visors and 1 band 1⅛in (2.8cm) by 11in (27.9cm).

C2. CARDBOARD (a heavy manila folder): Cut 1 piece of cardboard ½in (1.3cm) by 11in (27.9cm) for cap band and 1 visor.

C3. WIRE: Cut 1 piece of No. 21 milliner's wire 11in (27.9cm) long.

C4. CROWN LINING: Cut 1 crown lining of a dark cotton fabric.

CAP ASSEMBLY
H1. Cardboard band: Bring ends of cardboard together and glue, overlapping 1in (2.5cm), to form a circle. Using ½in (1.3cm) bias, glue ¼in (.65cm) around INSIDE edge of band, and overlap. Remaining ¼in (.65cm) extended will be flipped up to hold wire in place. Shape wire to fit OUTSIDE of band, overlap ends and secure by gluing lightly and wrapping end with heavy thread.

H2. WIRE: Slide circle of wire over band, at edge where bias strip is extended — a little glue will help hold wire in place, making sure wire remains exactly at bottom edge of band.

H3. LEATHER: Center leather band over cardboard stretching slightly to fit, overlap and glue ends; then turn extra leather to inside of top and bottom of band and glue in place. Remember that wire marks the bottom of the band.

H4. CROWN: Glue crown lining to underside of crown, using light layer of glue. Let dry. Mark *crown* and *brim* in quarters. Using the WIDE curve of the brim, fit around the circular crown, matching quarter-marks, right sides together. Whip crown to brim with tiny stitches and a VERY NARROW seam allowance. It may be necessary to hold circle in slightly to fit.

FITTING BRIM TO BAND
H5. Matching quarter marks of band and brim (the narrow inside curve of the brim), glue in place the seam allowance, fitting seam allowance inside the band.

VISOR
H6. Clip inside curve of cardboard visor at ¼in (.65cm) intervals as shown on pattern. Using the thumb of glove, glue it to the underside of the visor. Trim leather even with front edge of visor, smoothing leather with fingers and leave a ¼in (.65cm) extension around inside curve of visor beyond the cardboard.

H7. Using second thumb of glove, glue to top of visor, cutting leather to fit the inside curve of the cardboard, and leave *uncovered* the clipped edge of the cardboard (this will fit under the hatband when visor is attached).

H8. Trim extension of glove leather around the outside edge of visor to ⅛in (.31cm) extension. Lightly glue this extension and fold over to underbrim. This will make a neat rolled edge on the visor. LAST! Lightly glue the cardboard still visible and fit under the band, holding securely in place until set. With care in this step, no cardboard will be visible either on the inside or the outside of this beautiful little cap.

CAP TRIM
H9. Form a piece of round braid into a long figure 8 just large enough to fit on visor, and hold in place at each end with buttons to match suit.

NOTE: The design of this cap is such that the brim forms a natural curve falling slightly over the band.

This adds a truly professional touch to the entire costume, and if you are using leather you will be particularly delighted with the results..well worth the labor. Good luck!

SHOES: High boots, laced, typical of boys' wear in 1880s to 1890s.

FABRIC: Heavy leather.

By using heavy leather, holes can be pierced for laces without necessity of using reinforcement or eyelets.

INSTRUCTIONS FOR MAKING SHOES
S1. Of heavy leather cut 2 uppers. Lay pattern on wrong side of leather. In ink draw a line around border of pattern. BEFORE cutting, machine-stitch around upper edges and down centerfront with thread matching leather, ⅛in (.31cm) from marked line. THEN: Cut on marked line.

S2. Of cardboard (dark manila folder), cut 4 soles. If preferred, a tablet-back may be used for 2 stiffer innersoles.

S3. Of unbleached muslin, cut 2 soles, ¼in (.65cm) wider than sole pattern. Using the 2 innersoles, glue cardboard lightly and place muslin over soles, smoothing carefully. Fold excess muslin over edges of cardboard and glue.

S4. UPPERS: Punch holes as indicated on pattern using an awl which produces a hole about the size of a pinhead.
MAKE LACES 13in (33cm) long..use 4 strands of sewing thread, about 54in (137.1cm) for each of the 2 laces.

S5. SEW CENTERFRONT SEAM OF UPPERS. Put laces in shoes, ready for fitting. To facilitate inserting laces, use either a crochet hook or tapestry needle.

S6. Fit innersole on doll's foot, holding in place with rubber bands. Place upper on doll's foot (over sox) and tighten laces. Check fit at centerback. If shoe upper appears to be too large, adjustment may be made by cutting and seaming at centerback.

S7. Set upper over innersole (muslin side up) matching centerback and centerfront, ¼in (.65cm) lapping over edge. Apply glue on this edge and fold over innersole. You may clip seam allowance around curves, or work leather in place with fingers.

S8. OUTER SOLE: Curve edges upward slightly around pencil, sand edges a little, then glue over innersole. A little leather may be inserted between soles before completing the gluing process to keep soles level. THAT'S ALL!

FOR SIZE 19in (48.3cm) DOLL SHOES:

NO PATTERN is given for the larger doll, but the 17in (43.2cm) pattern may be enlarged easily. Cut soles for 19in (48.3cm) doll, adding to length and width as necessary. Extend at centerback when cutting uppers, to accommodate the larger size, and follow all instructions given for the 17in (43.2cm) shoe.

PATTERN FOR BOY'S SAILOR SUIT
SIZE 19in (48.3cm) DOLL

Pattern 2

This little sailor suit, adapted from *The Delineator,* September 1885, by Hazel Ulseth and Helen Shannon, consists of long, slightly bell-bottomed pants with a fall-front opening. The top is slightly bloused and has a typical sailor collar coming to a point at centerfront, around a striped dickey. Rows of crocheted chain in red provide color contrast on collar, cuffs, pocket and belt. A broad round sailor hat matches the suit and has red trim, also. A belt with red trim completes the suit.

FABRIC SUGGESTIONS:

See information on pattern for 17in (43.2cm) doll.

FABRIC REQUIREMENTS

Waist: Small pieces of muslin.
Suit and Hat: 36in (91.4cm) by 27in (68.6cm) or
45in (114.3cm) by 24in (61cm).

CUTTING INSTRUCTIONS

PANTS

Cl. *Lining.* Cut 2 fronts, 2 backs.
Suiting fabric. Cut 2 fronts, 2 backs, 1 front facing, 4 fallbearers.

WAIST...of lining fabric

C2. *Suiting fabric.* Cut 2 fronts, 1 back, 2 front facings and 1 back facing (see lines on pattern) 1

flap 1¼in (3.2cm) by 5¼in (13.4cm) and 1 band 1¼in (3.2cm) by 14in (35.6cm).
Dickey (referred to by *The Delineator* as a vest). Cut 2 of contrasting fabric.

BLOUSE

C3. *Suiting fabric.* Cut 2 fronts, 1 back, 2 front facings and 1 back facing (see lines on pattern) 2 collars, 2 sleeves, 4 cuffs, 1 belt, 1 pocket.

SAILOR HAT

For a less floppy hat, crown and brim may be lined, either with lightweight cotton or fusible lining. For this doll a lightweight cotton jersey was used.

C4. *Lining.* Cut 1 crown and 1 brim.
PLEASE NOTE: It is difficult to name parts of hats. For convenience we have used CROWN to designate the top circle of the hat and BRIM for the lower circular section.
Suiting fabric. Cut 1 crown, 1 brim and 1 band 4in (10.2cm) by 14in (35.6cm). Note that 1 crown is to be cut of pattern given and the brim is the same size, to be cut from the same pattern, but with a small inner circle removed, as noted on pattern.
Cardboard. Cut 1 band, ½in (1.3cm) by 13in (33cm).
Muslin. Cut 1 band 1¼in (3.2cm) by 13in (33cm).

Illustration No. 1

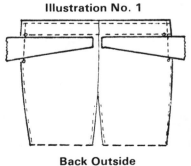

Back Outside

Illustration No. 2

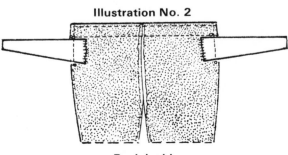

Back Inside

ASSEMBLY INSTRUCTIONS

PANTS (11½in (29.2cm) waistline)

A1. LINING. Placing front pants and back pants on corresponding lining pieces, baste all around.

A2. Matching notches, machine-stitch centerfront seam and press open.

A3. FACE FRONT of PANTS. Clip corners of lower front facing and press upward on seam allowance. Place front facing on front pants, right sides together, machine-stitching around from o.......o. Clip side seams as shown on pattern; turn right sides out and press. Sew facing flat, tacking to lining.

A4. Matching notches, machine-stitch centerback seam.

A5. FALLBEARER. Place each pair of fallbearers right sides together; sew around 3 sides as shown on pattern. Turn right sides out and press. See *Illustration No. 1* (page 111).

A6. Matching notches, place fallbearers on back pants, right sides together, and machine-stitch on seam allowance, from o.......o. See *Illustration No. 2* (page 111).

A7. SIDE SEAMS and CROTCH SEAMS. Matching notches, sew side seams. Press open. Repeat for crotch seams.

A9. LAP FALLBEARERS. Lap at centerfront line and close with buttons or hooks and eyes.

A10. ATTACH FALL (top of pants front), to fallbearers by 4 hooks and eyes at side seams.

A11. HEM. (If lining is heavy, cut off at seamline.) Check length of pants on doll; then turn hem and tack in place.

WAIST FOR SAILOR BLOUSE

A12. Matching notches, sew shoulder seams and side seams and press open using flap, fold ends in ¼in (.65cm) and tack. Fold flap lengthwise and baste to right side of waist front, raw edges matching.

A13. WAIST FACING. Sew shoulder seams and press open. Place facing on two fronts and around back neck edge, covering flap in front. Machine-stitch, clip to stitching around back of neck, turn, press and tack flat, leaving flap out toward centerfront. For closure, attach hooks on left side of waist and eyes at seam line where facing is joined.

A14. DICKEY. Place right sides together, machine-stitch from o.......o, turn right sides out, press and blindstitch opening. Dickey should be attached to waist, the right side hand-sewn on line shown on pattern, the left side attached with snap fasteners on left waist front.

A15. BLOUSE. Machine-stitch shoulder seams and side seams; press seams open. Machine-stitch 2 rows of gathering threads around bottom of blouse ¼in (.65cm) apart. Complete pocket and sew in place on blouse.

A16. BLOUSE COLLAR. Matching notches with right sides together, sew around outside, leaving neck seam open. Turn right sides out and press along seam line. Baste a stay-stitch line around neck edge.

Collar should be trimmed at this point with rows of red trim as shown on picture. (See A25 for TRIM.)

Lay collar on blouse, matching centerback and centerfront of collar. Baste in place along blouse front and neck edge.

A17. ATTACH FACING. Using facings cut of suiting fabric, machine-stitch shoulder seams and press open. Turn edge under ¼in (.65cm) and tack. Lay facing over collar and down centerfronts. Machine-stitch facing in place, turn to inside, press and tack. Sew 4 hooks and eyes down centerfront as shown on pattern.

A18. ATTACH BLOUSE TO WAIST. Set blouse over waist, matching shoulder seams and side seams. Tack shoulder seams and back neck edge and baste around matching armseyes. Matching lower sideseams, centerbacks and centerfronts, pull gathering stitches of blouse to fit waist, distribute evenly and baste in place. NOTE that blouse is longer than the waist to provide the "blousing" effect.

A19. WAISTLINE. Using the cut strip of muslin 1¼in (3.2cm) by 14in (35.6cm), fold lengthwise and machine-stitch both ends. Turn right sides out and press. Lay this along blouse bottom on the right side, with raw edges matching. It should fit waist perfectly. Machine-stitch in place. Turn band DOWN and seam allowance UP. Tack seam allowance to waist only, leaving blouse free of stitches. Close band with hook and eye.

A20. ATTACH PANTS TO BLOUSE. Using hooks and eyes, sew eyes at top of band, and matching hooks on pants to hold pants in place. If pants fit your doll perfectly, this may not be necessary.

SLEEVES

A21. SLEEVES. Place sleeve linings on corresponding sleeves and baste all around (OPTIONAL). Pin sleeve seams, machine-stitch to o, and press seams open, turning seam allowance for small placket opening and tack. Machine-stitch 2 rows of gathering stitches between notches at top of sleeve (for shaping) and around bottom edge.

A22. CUFFS. Place 2 cuffs right side together (2 each of four pieces) and sew 3 sides. Turn right sides out and press. Place one edge of cuff on sleeve, right sides together, pull gathering stitches to fit and hand-stitch in place. Turn other edge of cuff ¼in (.65cm) and tack in place. Trim. (See A25 for TRIM). Close with hooks and threaded loops.

A23. Fit sleeves into armseye, matching notches. Use gathering threads to cup sleeve at shoulder and to achieve good fit. Baste sleeves in place and fit blouse on doll. Hand-stitch sleeves in place.

BELT

A24. Cut a strip of suiting fabric 1½in (3.8cm) by 16in (40.6cm), fold with right sides together and sew long end and one short end. Turn right side out and press, trim with rows of stitching (See A25. TRIM), and add a buckle.

TRIM

A25. TRIM FOR SAILOR SUIT. Use on collar, belt, cuffs, pocket and hatband.

FOUR OPTIONS for TRIM...or try something on your own.

1. Using medium zigzag, zigzag over 4 strands of embroidery thread..OR
2. Using embroidery floss, embroider a chain stitch..OR
3. Using embroidery floss, embroider an outline stitch..OR
4. Make chain-trim by crocheting 4 strands of embroidery thread and press before applying to garment. Attach with embroidery thread by hand.

NECK BOW

A26. A small ribbon bow may be attached at intersection of collar. Bosun's whistle may be attached with very narrow twisted cord.

AND ON TO THE SAILOR'S HAT!

SAILOR BOY'S HAT FOR 19in (48.3cm) DOLL (Head circumference for 11¾in [29.9cm] head)

ASSEMBLY

H1. HATBAND, Carefully bend cardboard into a circle, overlap ½in (1.3cm) and glue in place. Stitch 21 gauge milliners wire (or floral wire) on outside edge of cardboard. Wired edge is bottom of hatband. Using muslin strip glue to outside of cardboard, centering cardboard to leave equal amounts of fabric on each side of cardboard. Fold excess fabric to inside of top and bottom. Glue in place.

H2. Using hatband of suiting, fold in half lengthwise and press. Sew 4 rows of trim (See A25) starting the first row ⅝in (1.6cm) from fold, and continuing with the second row a little less than ⅛in (.31cm) from the first. Complete 2 more rows of trim using exactly ½in (1.3cm) in all (to cover the hatband). Glue trimmed hatband to hatband base (the cardboard) making sure trim fits the outside edges. Fold over excess fabric at TOP of band and glue to inside.(Let excess fabric at bottom of band remains loose for the moment.)

CROWN and BRIM

H3. Lining. If lining is desired, it should be applied to crown and brim at this point.

H4. Staystitch. Staystitch on seamline around inner circle. Clip to machine-stitching at ½in (1.3cm) intervals.

H5. Combining CROWN and BRIM. Baste outer edges of circles, right sides together; then machine stitch. Press open this seam, a little at a time, and machine-stitch ⅛in (.31cm) on each side of seamline. This will serve to round out the edge. Divide hatband baste and the inner circle in quarters, marking with tiny safety pins. Matching safety pins, fit seam allowance into band, pin and glue into band. Let dry.

Turn remaining excess fabric up and into band, glue in place, covering seam allowance of brim.

A DARLING HAT...AND YOU HAVE DONE IT!

NOTES

NOTES

NOTES

NOTES

NOTES

Antique Children's Fashions 1880-1900
by Hazel Ulseth & Helen Shannon

A comprehensive reference guide for doll costumers features making and trimming doll costumes and their accessories plus instructions on patterns. Make authentic costumes for French Bébé's and German bisques of the late 19th century. Featured is a full-size pattern for a 20½ inch (52.1cm) doll plus a Fashion Plate section reproduced from *The Delineator* magazine 1880-1900. Additional sections on hats, shoes, trims, underwear, ribbons, bows and much more. 20 color photographs of full length costumes. 125 pages. Paper $12.95

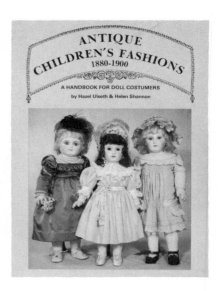

Costume Cameos I
by Hazel Ulseth & Helen Shannon

Recreate a splendid 18in (45.7cm) antique doll's outfit from the original 1887 pattern. Outfit includes a guimpe with skirt and suspenders (BRETELLE), a fashionable Scottish hat, and an 1898 girls sunbonnet. Fashion illustrations will serve as inspiration for doll dresser's who desire variations, instructions on utilizing the antique techniques of "How to Do Cartridge Pleating," and "How to Do Ribbons" will aide in creating doll heirloom outfits. $3.95

Doll Reader
Make and Dress
Volume I
edited by Virginia Heyerdahl

The Doll Reader magazine has compiled a series of doll making and dressing articles divided into four parts featuring over 50 projects. The sections include doll making (cloth, wooden, a Queen Anne, pincushion, and 10 other doll projects); doll costumes and patterns (outfits for French fashion lady dolls, doll shoes and bonnets, plus 35 other projects); miniature needlework projects; and finally, repairing and restoring articles by experts. 203 pages, 8⅜ x 10½ inches. Paper. $9.95

Available at
Distinctive Doll Shops & Bookstores
or directly from
the publisher

Hobby House Press, Inc.

900 Frederick Street, Dept. CC
Cumberland, Maryland 21502

Costume Cameos II
by Hazel Ulseth & Helen Shannon

Dress a 19in (48.3cm) doll in the height of Victorian fashion. Adapted from a child's dress and bonnet pattern from the 1898 edition of *The Delineator*, the authors offer a doll costume with all the frills and furbelows of that exotic period - shoes, bonnet trimmings and fringing. Additional patterns for making a sitting bear in two sizes and paper dolls are also included. $3.95